He Gave Me His Heart, So I Gave Him Mine

A Persian Pilgrim's Journey from Islam's Kingdom of Darkness to the Son's Kingdom of Light

Dr. Showkat Alborzi

WESTBOW PRESS®
A DIVISION OF THOMAS NELSON
& ZONDERVAN

Copyright © 2016 Dr. Showkat Alborzi.

All rights reserved. No part of this book may be used or reproduced by any means, graphic, electronic, or mechanical, including photocopying, recording, taping or by any information storage retrieval system without the written permission of the author except in the case of brief quotations embodied in critical articles and reviews.

WestBow Press books may be ordered through booksellers or by contacting:

WestBow Press
A Division of Thomas Nelson & Zondervan
1663 Liberty Drive
Bloomington, IN 47403
www.westbowpress.com
1 (866) 928-1240

Because of the dynamic nature of the Internet, any web addresses or links contained in this book may have changed since publication and may no longer be valid. The views expressed in this work are solely those of the author and do not necessarily reflect the views of the publisher, and the publisher hereby disclaims any responsibility for them.

Any people depicted in stock imagery provided by Thinkstock are models, and such images are being used for illustrative purposes only.
Certain stock imagery © Thinkstock.

ISBN: 978-1-4908-9548-2 (sc)
ISBN: 978-1-4908-9550-5 (hc)
ISBN: 978-1-4908-9549-9 (e)

Print information available on the last page.

WestBow Press rev. date: 01/08/2016

To my Lily:

Whose heart reminds me of the tenderness of my Savior's heart,

Whose beautiful face is the reflection of my Father's glory,

Whose forgiving nature resembles the compassion of the Son,

Whose name captures the sweet fragrance of the Lily of the Valley,

Whose every heartbeat, every smile,

Testifies of the Spirit's promise—" . . . by His stripes, we are healed."

For we both bear "the marks of Jesus."

CONTENTS

ACKNOWLEDGMENTS ix
INTRODUCTION xi

1. The Early Years 1
   My Father—the Mountain-Born..3
   My Mother—the Flower-Born 13

2. God Really Exists! 16

3. Revolutions—Small and Big 29
   My Small Revolution...37
   My Country's Big Revolution 41

4. America—the Other End of the Earth 45
   My Father's Visit 52
   Off to the Next Waypoint..54

5. When It Rains, It Pours! 57

6. Betrayed . . . Big Time!..68
   Truth Distorted 72
   The Falsehood of Islam...73
      I. Allah—a False God..75
      II. Mohammed—a False Prophet 82
      III. Qur'an—a False Doctrine.....................................92

7. Showers of Blessings 100
   Paid in Full..100
   The Return Ticket 102
   Healed by His Stripes at 4:00 a.m. 103
   Tech Support from the Great Engineer 105
   "The Life of Christ" in an Antique Shop......................106
   Happy Birthday, My Child! 107
   It Was Lost, but Now It's Found 109

    Pray Like Jesus 110
    Jesus at the Wheel on I-495 111
    "Name that Book" from Thirty Thousand Feet 113
    I Didn't Let You Go 114
        Only You, Jesus 115

8. **Turning Strongholds into Reasons to Believe** 117
    Stronghold 1: The Bible, "Injil," Was Written by Men,
    Not God, and Is Corrupted/Changed 118
        The Word of God or Man's Opinion? 119
        Is the Bible Corrupted/Changed? 121
    Stronghold 2: Jesus Is a Mere Prophet, Not the Son of God 123
    Stronghold 3: The Trinity—God Is One, Not Three! 126
    Stronghold 4: The Crucifixion 127
    Stronghold 5: The Resurrection 129
    Stronghold 6: The Sin 130
    Stronghold 7: Leaving Islam 134
    Pray to Receive Jesus as Your Lord and Savior 136
    My Personal Prayer 136

ACKNOWLEDGMENTS

I would like to express my gratitude to the following people whose valuable contributions have made this book possible.

To Chaplain Luther Alexander, US Navy captain (ret.), for his support and editing of my manuscript, as well as for his love, care, and encouragement.

To Tim Huddleston, for his continuous love and friendship. The Son's light shines through your confident smile and your humbled heart. I will never forget our Tuesday-evening studies of the book of John, our mission trip to Ukraine, and our time around the dinner table recalling all those awesome-God stories!

To Sam and Lisa Capitano for sharing the love of Christ with me (over crispy rice and tea) in my early days in Virginia.

To Pastor Skip Heitzig, whose teaching of God's Word is second to none! He is truly our "treasured inheritance"! Special thanks to Mark and Deanna Pilcher, whose fellowship during my trips to Albuquerque has been a priceless gift from the great Giver of gifts.

And my wholehearted thanks to the Expound Bible study group: Sam, John, Phil, Pastor Justin, and my fellow "traitor" Joel. I have learned so much from you all. God bless the entire Calvary of Albuquerque Church for all you do to make disciples of all nations.

To Pastor Tom and Linda Strode for your love and care throughout past years.

To Pastor Michael and Jeannine Reid and my friends at the Temple Baptist Church for their love and tireless service to proclaim the truth.

To my children, whose pursuit of the truth is not only my greatest joy, it is the crown of my life given to me by the King of kings, and to my daughter-in-law, who shares my "weakness" for the cross!

My honey-sweetened thanks are given to my granddaughter, Lily, who kept me on schedule and reminded me every night of my deadline to finish this book. Her nighttime prayers for the book were not only sweet in His ears but also a source of strength for my daily weariness.

INTRODUCTION

I am the light of the world. Whoever follows me will never walk in darkness, but will have the light of life.
—John 8:12

Imagine that you are wandering hopelessly, confused by the wilderness you live in, stumbling at times, in search of your home. The dryness of the wilderness resembles the desolate desert of *Dasht-e-Kavir*. Although you pass by multitude of people—young and old, rich and poor, clean and unclean, educated or unschooled—you feel as alone as if you were the only human being on earth. You are weary and doubtful of your future. Your mind is pounded with questions: Will I ever find my way home? Will I be safe and secure? Will I be able to counter any troubles along the way? How did I get lost? Is my father looking for me? Or am I fatherless, motherless, and totally alone?

Questions inflate in your mind, and so you let go of thinking and just concentrate on walking. Life has become mere survival, and living has lost its meaning. The darkness of the night adds an additional element of loneliness and emptiness to this mere existence. You question your sanity: Is this just my mind playing games with me? Or is this life as it really is?

You are desperately thirsty and hungry, but you finished all the food and drink you had stored in your backpack. You are faced with the bitter reality that there is no replenishment in sight. The backpack is heavy and is weighing you down. Though you have no food or drink left, you are holding on to your backpack obsessively; in it, you have stored years of possessions, events, and memories. It represents your life and all that you own.

The unbearable hot sun is scorching your skin, but you cannot hide your face from it. As far as eye can see is a vast dry land and no sign of home. Your lower back is hurting and bent forward; the pain is unbearable. Your feet refuse to take another step.

Your eyes are open, but you cannot see. The patterns of darkness sweep before you and attempt to distract you from focusing on your destination. People seem to not notice when they bump into you as they walk along their way. The void of joy in their faces makes you question your own face: What does my face tell the world? What do my eyes convey? Am I totally blind, or am I blind only to the reality that I am searching for? Are we all seeing the same thing, or is it possible that with my open eyes, I am yet blind, and that is perhaps why I am lost and can't find my way home?

Everywhere you look seems strange. People seem to not see your desperate state. The darkness beyond your eyes weighs heavily on your shoulders. Knowing how inadequately you are equipped, you wonder about the reality in which you live. Innocently, you turn your blind eyes upward in a plea for help.

Then, imagine that a great hand comes out of nowhere, lifts you up and puts you on the other side of the barren desert, and you know you have arrived to safety! Oh, and in this safety, you don't need your backpack; you have everything you would ever need right there—streams of pure cool water that can quench any thirst forever, warm and fresh bread that satisfies any hunger, completely and permanently, and the embrace of a bright and shining day that lasts till the end of ages. Your backache is now a faded memory, and pain has no meaning. And the tears, those tears of sadness and of loneliness are wiped away. And best of all, you can see! The world is no longer hanging in total vulnerability on its own. Life is not just a one-dimensional physical existence, ready to be cut away by your enemies, but in fact it is tied to an unbreakable anchor. A new life has just begun. You measure your worth in a totally new way than before. And above all, your Father is waiting for you with arms open wide!

Oh, yes, you are definitely home, safe and sound.

The deep sigh of relief comes out of your soul and you look up to the heavens and say, "Grace carried me here, grace brought me to safety."

This is precisely my story.

This book intends to record a personal journey from an empty, directionless life to a life of purpose, riches, and joy; a journey from total darkness to pure light; a journey from a living death to a life eternal.

This book is my personal testimony of God's love and faithfulness—immeasurable love, for it extends to infinity and beyond. This book records my personal experiences, understanding, and interpretation of events and facts in my life as a former Muslim. It records a young Persian girl's genuine and sincere desire to find her Creator, to find her own true identity, her beginning as well as her destiny according to her Maker's design rather than according to her own thoughts and understandings.

My testimonial journey began in Iran when God first showed me His character of love in a very real, tangible, physical, and practical way. I believe this was done to distinguish Himself from the false, abstract, angry, and ready-to-punish god called Allah, to whom we gave prayers born of obligation. Then He took me through several life events and enduring times that lasted twenty years but always left me with an imprint of His hand and His nearness, or at minimum, an indicator by which I could pulse myself and know that I was on the right track on my walk toward Him and toward His truth. And finally, as if we were in a boxing ring, He released His most powerful punch and knocked me down totally! That "fatal" knockdown left me with no doubt of who the true God is and who is the truth and the way. That was the moment of truth—the moment I believed.

My journey was long and difficult but rich in learning and discovery. The path was bumpy, filled with stumbling blocks of centuries-old rituals and dos and don'ts, deep potholes of sadness and mourning over past betrayals, and inconvenient detours such as religious guilt trips, lies, and superstitions.

But thankfully, the destination was the truth—the truth of life! This is the truth that set me free: free from the bondage of sin, free from worldly strongholds, free from religion, free from guilt and shame, free and safe in the arms of Prince of Peace for all eternity.

I am convinced that if we really want the ultimate truth of life, we can have it just by asking the truth to reveal itself. Some of you may laugh and ask, "how could you ask the truth to reveal itself?" I say to you, because the ultimate truth is a person! He hears you, acts on your request, and He will reveal the truth—that is, reveal Himself to you.

Those who deny or question the existence of God, the deity of Christ, His redemptive work on the cross, or His resurrection are the ones who spend little or no time seeking the truth. In my opinion, in their deepest core of conscience, they know they cannot handle the truth. So they avoid it; it seems so much easier. It's easier because truth demands action. Truth demands a response. Truth comes with accountability. Truth needs to be handled appropriately and proclaimed as such. Most importantly, truth matters.

Last year an old high school friend of mine from Iran called in the middle of the night to congratulate me on the Persian New Year—*Nowruz*. I told her that I was tired and went to sleep early because I had been busy at the church.

"Church?" she asked. "I didn't know you changed your religion to Christianity."

"I didn't change religions," I said. "Many years ago, I found the true God and I gave my heart and my life to Him. I am a Christian now. It's not a religion, it's a relationship, a very close kinship with God."

"They are all the same, right? Islam and Christianity?" she asked.

"Actually," I answered, "there is a difference the size of eternity!"

She didn't understand.

Yes, grace carried me to the other side of my personal Dead Sea that had separated me from my Father and my home.

There on the other side, I was born anew. Darkness was no more, for the light of the Son brightened my days and the peace of the Prince of Peace began to reign in my new life. The dark and tarnished forces could not pull me away or hold me captive. The emptiness of my heart suddenly was filled with a running river of life as sweet and pure as the utterance of the name of Jesus from the lips of a babe.

Like a caged bird being freed for the first time, I flapped my wings harder, faster and flew higher to feel, touch, and taste the truth. My Deliverer's words were music to my ears:

> *Those who hope in the Lord will renew their strength.*
> *They will soar on wings like eagles; they will run and*
> *not grow weary, they will walk and not be faint.*
> —Isaiah 40:31

My primary purpose for writing this book is to give thanks to the one and only Savior of the world for His awesome rescue of me.

The secondary purpose is to tell others about the ultimate truth of life. Once a person comes to the knowledge of this truth, hears its good news, touches its essence, tastes its fruit, and sees its life-giving properties, nothing less will do.

I must also state clearly what this book is not. This book is not intended to be an apologetic in nature, although where needed, I offered some apologies to drive my point. Additionally, it is not a biographical book either, but some biographical context is provided in support of my primary and secondary purposes.

Beloved Muslim brothers and sisters, especially those of you from Iran, I want to invite you and in fact, to challenge you to seek the truth. Don't be afraid. Those who stop you from reading the Holy Bible or prohibit you from asking questions about Jesus (or even about your own religion) have a personal agenda; they want to keep you uninformed, captive, and under their control!

The true God, however, wants you to be free. He wants you to hear His Word, to question it, and to discuss it with others. And most of all, He wants you to choose whom you believe in based on knowledge, understanding, and free will. God loves Iranian Muslims as much as He loves His chosen people of Israel.

> *God so loved the world, that He gave His only begotten son . . .*
> —*John 3:16*

Christ is for the whole world, not just for the Jews, Americans, or other Westerners. After His resurrection, Jesus asked His disciples to go to the whole *world* and tell them about His good news of salvation!

> *Go and make disciples of all nations . . .*
> —*Matthew 28:19*

Islam has been hiding many profound and consequential truths from the Muslims that hide the ultimate truth of life—that Jesus Christ is the Lord and Savior of the world, and we cannot have salvation (*amorzesh*) without Him.

> *Salvation is found in no one else, for there is no other name under heaven given to mankind by which we must be saved.*
> —*Acts 4:12*

Whosoever believes in Him shall not perish but have everlasting life.
—*John 3:16*

I pray that my testimony would invoke in you the fiery desire to seek, find, and know the true God for yourself. He has already promised that if we seek Him, we will find Him. This is not a maybe, not a "if you go to Mecca" or "if you observe the fasting and *namaz* rituals." This is Almighty God's promise to mankind!

> *You will seek me and find me when you seek me with all your heart. I will be found by you," declares the LORD, "and I will bring you back from captivity.*
> —*Jeremiah 29:11-14*

Lord, thank You for bringing me back from captivity!

—Showkat Alborzi

1

THE EARLY YEARS

You have been a refuge for the poor, a refuge for the needy in his distress, a shelter from the storm and a shade from the heat.
—Isaiah 25:4

Who knew that I would open my eyes to this world for the first time in the temple of Solomon! That is exactly where I was born and where spent the first ten years of my life. *Masjed-i-Soleiman,* or its English translation, "the temple of Solomon," is a small town in southern Iran that is unknown even to most Iranians. My neighborhood was like an ancient scene out of the Bible.

The water source in the center of the neighborhood was the main attraction. Women came with buckets to get water twice a day, sometimes fighting over whose turn it was. It was the place where they would visit each other daily to socialize and gossip and give or receive news. It was a place where they had their women talk.

We had a couple of large ceramic containers that held several liters of drinking water and were kept in the enclosed backyard (*hayat*) to stay cool for the day. The temperature in summer would reach 110 degrees Fahrenheit, and there were no refrigerators or air conditioners in homes.

The dirt and stony ground was the playground for the children of the neighborhood. We walked through the rocky roads and hills to go to school. There was a public restroom made up a few stalls, which were also situated in the center of the neighborhood, and a public bath that also served as an outing for the women. I remember a simple life that resembles only a dream today.

Everyone knew everyone else at least three generations back. People were introduced to others as the "son of" or "daughter of" someone. People knew the trail of ancestral names by that introduction. That is why individualism was a foreign concept for me when I came to the United States thirty-plus years ago. The family name was to be upheld with respect, integrity, and service because it had almost an eternal impact. Sometimes one's livelihood depended on that! People were given or denied jobs based on their family name. People were married or were refused in marriage based on their family name.

The meaning behind names was also important back then and there. My name means "glorious" or "glory," as in kingly or monarchial glory. My name was so classic and outdated that my parents picked a nickname to call me by, and that was my name except in schools, where they used the official legal name. Growing up, I didn't like my name because it wasn't a modern or a popular name, and it caused me embarrassment at school. It was decades later, when I came to know Christ, my Lord and King, that I loved my name. I thought it was appropriate that I, the daughter of the King of kings, was called glorious or Showkat. I have no doubt that He was in control of the selection of my name some fifty years ago in that unknown little village in the most unknown suburb town of Iran.

In my neighborhood, women even breastfed each other's children when needed. In the Middle East culture even to this day, when a mother breastfeeds another mother's baby, that baby and her own are considered siblings, and therefore cannot marry each other when they grow up. Such children were called milk-sisters or milk-brothers, denoting the root of their kinship.

Some years ago, when the first lady of the United States brought about the idea of "it takes a village to raise a child," I remembered my old childhood upbringing and culture. It wasn't a new idea for people who lived in the Middle East thirty or more years ago. A child was everyone's child, and people took care of each other. There were no governmental social services. People were each other's insurance and retirement resources. People often had their parents living with them.

I don't remember Islam having an active role in our lives, but people knew inherently that they were Muslims. It was just a fact of life, like being a southerner, a *Lor* (a tribe from the south), or a *Kurd* (a tribe from the northwest), etc. The only religious people in Khoozestan were those whose ancestors came from Arabia. Although the Qur'an was in every home, it was not an intimate part of one's life. There were no *personal* ties between people and the Qur'an as I was growing up.

In 1950s the British petroleum companies were very active in the south of Iran in drilling and producing crude oil and building refineries. Masjed-i-Soleiman is a small town in Khoozestan, a southern province that holds most of the country's oil. So although my town was an insignificant, underdeveloped little village, there were many British working there and supporting the economy by employing the local people, mostly for labor jobs. The British introduced to us the use of acronyms, specifically MIS for our town, since Persian words proved too difficult for them to pronounce. Local people started using the MIS too since it was a foreign word and therefore interesting!

My Father—the Mountain-Born

I had a wonderful childhood. My father was the rock of the family. His name in Farsi means "mountain-born." He was from a tribe called *Bakhtiari*, which are known for their bravery, generosity, and close kinships. This tribe would migrate with all their livestock in different seasons around the southwest parts of Iran based on weather. They were producers of dairy and meat and were self-sufficient. My favorite dairy product was *sar-shir*, a breakfast delight! I remember every time my aunt came to visit, she would bring canvas bags full of nuts, dried fruit, and berries. They were, and still are, one of the earliest and purest Persians in Iran.

Although the Bakhtiaris were Muslims by birth and by geography, they did not know much about the religion. They innocently would look at the clean, clear sky at nights with thousands of bright, winkling stars and pray to the Maker, although they couldn't tell you who the Maker was. Not knowing who the Maker is allows for superstitious activities. Islam was infested with superstitions, cults, *jinns*, and other unknown beings.

The laws governing the Bakhtiaris' lives were tribal laws. Their morality and ethics were also defined by the tribe. Often they intermarried to resolve wars, conflicts, etc. Although women, in general, were not as valuable as men, some women had power, influence, and wealth, and therefore were shakers and movers in the lives of the tribe.

My father lost both of his parents before he was twelve years old and was left to take care of himself and his three younger siblings. He worked during the day and went to school at night until ninth grade. Then he worked full time and started his own appliance-repair business.

My father was twenty-four years old when he married my mother. He was about ten years older than she was. According to my mother, my father waited a whole year before they consummated their marriage. The reason was one because she was too young and small in stature, and because my father wanted her to get to know him before getting intimate as man and wife. Western readers must know that in Islam, and at that time in Iran, if a husband did not consummate the marriage on his wedding night (or worse, if after), gossip and allegations of impotency would face him. It was a fate worse than death, for the shame and disgrace was unbearable by the families involved. I cannot recall of any man in the Islamic world who would be married legally with a legal-aged woman, live with her day in and day out, and yet wait one year to allow his wife to know him, to develop affection for him, and to grow in age and maturity, and only then consummate their marriage. This speaks of my father's high integrity and moral standing, even in his youth, and I must say, despite Islam.

He was also a visionary man with such an innovative and creative mind. With those characteristics, he was unstoppable!

I remember when I was about eight years old, to get relief from the heat, my father placed a big sheet of woven thorns and branches over an open door. He then rigged a garden hose atop the raft of branches so that the water would run from the top down. He placed a fan behind it and turned on the water; we had an instant air conditioner! It was so cool and pleasant that several of our neighbors would come to our house every day for an afternoon nap! Not everybody had a refrigerator. We were one of the first one to get one, but my father could not bear to see other families not able to cool themselves during the hot summer, so he shared his homemade air conditioner, refrigerator, and ice with others.

My father had an uncommon passion for serving others. A part of that passion was to serve the laborers by facilitating a good and fair working environment. He spoke for the voiceless and took initiative to establish or change work rules and regulations (there were no national labor laws, as I recall) to benefit the poor and middle-class people. The labor party elected him as their leader and as their official spokesman, and while in this capacity, he was able to officially establish labor laws for the local laborers that were systematic and fair to all. Fairness was (and still is) a rare commodity in Iran. He was a frontrunner in advocating fairness and justice in all facets of people's lives in the local areas where he was living and working. But he wanted to serve all the people of MIS, so he decided to run for the elected office in the Tehran's parliament representing his small hometown and won. He now was a *Namayandeh Majles*, equivalent to a US representative. His goal was to use his position and influence to help his people and elevate their quality of life.

During his tenure, he helped to build several schools, hospitals, roads, etc., for MIS and carried the burden of difficulties of life alongside his constituents. Once when the locals wanted to name a high school after him, he declined, and he suggested the name of one of the government's high officials who helped with the funding. He never sought money or fame for himself but worked to help the quality of life of the people.

He was a source of wisdom, strength, and perseverance for me. He loved his children and would go to the end of the world to provide for them. We did not have the type of Islamic mindset that Arab Muslims had. My father loved his three daughters! His friends and family used to accuse him of loving his daughters more than his five sons. My sister, who is two years older than me, was the apple of his eye! We all still retell the story of the time when she was in the third grade and came home one day with a red mark of a hand on her face. My father asked her what happened, and she told him that the teacher slapped her, apparently because she got into fight with another girl. My father went to the school the same day and made a complaint to the principal, and the teacher was severely disciplined. He helped the school to adopt a rule where no student could be physically disciplined or punished. This was unheard-of progress in a country that always had physical punishments (slaps, ruler, sometimes spanking), and it was a normal child-rearing and child-teaching method.

My fondest memory of him is when I was in high school and had a beginning course in English. He wanted me to learn all that the chapter contained, not just what the teacher would be testing us on, so when I asked him to practice the dictation with me—that is, testing the spelling of words—I had to study hard and beyond my textbook's lesson because he expected excellence and mastery of the material. Because of the love and respect I had for him, I wanted to please him as much as possible, so I would study the lessons teacher expected, *plus* I would go beyond those lessons and try to learn the spelling of all the words in the chapter! He taught me how not to limit myself to what teacher teaches and to go beyond.

I still remember a day when I was pacing in my room and was repeating the English letters, "T-H-A-N-K-Y-O-U." He heard me from a different room and said out loud, "Thank you?" I said yes. He was always at work with us.

His term of endearment for me was, *"Madarami, khaharami, dokhtarami,"* which literally means, "You're my mother, you're my sister, you're my daughter." In the Persian culture, especially the Bakhtiaris, there are three highest, almost sacred, relationships in any man's life. These are the relationships with one's mother, sister, and daughter. They are to be revered, loved, and supported by a man till the last day of his life. My father would pick my cheeks and would say this term of endearment. To him, I was as dear and valued as if I were all those three women for him!

My sister and I also remember a day in elementary school where both of us received two beautiful red vases as prizes for having performed at the top of our class. We noticed that no one else got awards other than a paper award, and we were pleased and knew that our parents were proud! It was ten or so years later during a family discussion that my mother told us that my father had bought those prizes himself and asked the principal to present them to us because he was very pleased with us and wanted to honor our hard work.

When I reflect back on these early years, I see the first time that God's hand on me was visible.

I was only seven years old, and I came down with typhoid. There were no vaccinations in a small town like MIS in those days. A lot of people died because of the childhood diseases. The likelihood of surviving this illness was dependent partly on the age, so the young children almost always died of it. I was in the hospital for over a month, and I was not showing any signs of recovery. I remember how thirsty I was! But apparently water was not good for me.

The hospital had only two hours of visitation in the afternoon, and no one was allowed in after the visitation period. My mother used to sneak in every few hours—even outside the visitation period—and smuggle me a handful of crushed ice. She would also clean my pillow so I wouldn't see how much hair I was losing.

My father would come to my side straight from work, and if they didn't let him, he would walk straight to the head of the hospital and protest the uncompassionate rules so they would let him come in. By the end of one month's hospitalization, the doctors lost all hope for my recovery. They told my father that they couldn't help any longer. The odds were against me. I was slowly dying, but my father did not give up.

The telephone was a new technology then. It was in a primitive state and could only be used by a few privileged officials. My father stormed to the office of high-ranking official in the oil company there and asked to use the phone. He called all the medical experts from neighboring provinces. He was convinced that this was a limitation of our small town—the lack of good doctors. Finally he found a doctor who was willing to come to our town. The doctor came and took over the direction of my treatment, and soon I got better, and after a few more weeks, I was totally well.

My father never forgot that doctor's willingness to come to a small town. He never forgot the doctor's efforts and expertise that saved my life. Later, when I was a teen, I learned that every year my father would visit the doctor's grave and thank him for giving him back his daughter. Looking back now, I know that God was behind it all and wanted me to live because He had a plan for me. As a Christian, I read the beautiful verse of Jeremiah 29:11-12: "'For I know the plans I have for you,' declares the LORD, 'plans to prosper you and not to harm you, plans to give you hope and a future.'" As I read it, I remembered this early event when God chose life for me when many others with the same disease died. I regret that my wonderful father did not know who really saved my life and whom he needed to thank first!

His first term in the parliament was a blast for us. We lived in Tehran, the capital, and it was different than MIS. Tehran was a big city with streetlights, traffic, and many tall buildings. The city was bright, with colorful and flashing lights at night.

We did not see my father much because he often traveled to MIS for all the projects he was involved in to elevate the standard of living in his hometown and serve the people by attending to their needs. During those four years, several schools, hospitals, and roads were built. The town experienced the biggest makeover anyone had ever seen. He made sure everyone had clean, piped water. He made sure everyone had electricity, air conditioners, central heat, etc. When he would make a trip to any site, people, especially women, would find their way close to him and hand him a piece of paper, usually a request for help with a problem they had. He would read all the requests and resolve them one by one.

A woman once handed him a paper that said her husband was put in jail unjustly and the charges were drugs related. She wrote that he was the source of income for her and their children and now they were hungry and could not live without the income. She requested that my father look into his case. My father investigated the man's case, talked to a lot of people, and looked into the charges, and he was able to expose the truth and the innocence of the man. He was freed and returned to his family. That family, for the next fifteen years or so, was the first to send us New Year cards and always thanked my father for his help that saved his family. Stories like these were numerous.

After one term in the parliament, my father won the second term by a landslide, but his name was struck out by the higher ups in the government, and another person's name was read on the official announcement of the winners. My father knew that he was the winner, but the government did not want him anymore because he was too popular among people and too generous with the government's money. Any popular person posed a threat!

He was very disappointed and took the loss very hard. We realized decades later that this was God's will, and it was a good thing that he did not win the second term.

We moved back to Khoozestan, and my father found employment with the National Iranian Oil Company (NIOC) as a manager.

About fifteen years later, the storm of the Islamic Revolution shook Iran, and the new regime executed thousands of the shah's staff, senators, and representatives going back several terms. They started with those who were elected for more than one term. They knew that if a person was in the parliament more than one term, he or she must have been a supporter of the shah since the shah had allowed the reelection.

The new regime came after my father too. They summoned him to Tehran for questioning periodically for six years. My father told them the truth. He told them how he worked for the people and how he elevated the people's quality of life in just four years and how the shah did not allow him to be reelected despite people's unanimous vote. He told them that he did not accumulate wealth because his loyalty was directed to the country and to the people. They interrogated him, investigated, and searched for any evidence of special ties to the monarchy. An example of evidence would be an accumulation of wealth. The new regime finally gave up because they did not find any evidence of wealth, special privileges, etc., and they cleared him. Our family realized that if my father had been chosen the second term, he would have been executed quickly, without any trial.

The Qur'an is devoid of logic for comfort purposes, but the Holy Bible makes this story a sensible one: *"A generous man will prosper; he who refreshes others will himself be refreshed"* (Prov. 11:25).

In the last few months of his life, he came to the United States to see me as well as his grandchildren, whom he had never seen before. He was battling colon cancer, and so this visit was his last wish. He stayed a couple of months, long enough to become a memory in my children's minds.

I remember how he was impressed at the order and peace of the United States. He would look out of the window of his room and smile at the orderly, mild traffic. He would stare at the cars stopping quietly and slowly at stop signs (without anyone watching them) and people walking by and saying hi to each other or to the owners of houses. No one seemed to bother anyone, and the calm and peace were overwhelming. He would observe closely everything, and he would shake his head with regret that his country fell into hands of the new regime that wiped out any hope of progress it might have ever had. As a child who weeps for the loss of a parent, he wept for the loss of Iran. He didn't blame it on Islam but on people who "falsely" testified of it. I did not know the truth then, so I did not offer any consolation.

My last memory of him is when he wept at the airport and asked me to forgive him for anything that he had ever done that may have caused a pain or resentment in me. I told him that there was nothing there to forgive but that I needed his forgiveness for all that I had done in the past that was displeasing to him. He didn't have strength to use words but cried and kissed my face and left. I waited to see his plane leave the area. I even took a picture of the plane right before it left the gate. I knew that I would never see him again. He died a few months later at his home in Iran at the age of sixty-two. His loss was mourned by thousands of people who over the course of forty-plus years somehow benefitted from his services and his kindness.

My mother told me later that in the last year of his battle with cancer, he searched for a spiritual answer because he knew death was coming. He sought the counsel of a few elder spiritual men. My father thought that they might know of why he was suffering and why he has lost all his body mass to this disease even though he had served humanity all his life. He didn't understand why God seemed to punish him with this cancer in spite of his service to many people and all of the sacrifices he made for others. He recalled that even the constituents from other provinces came for help to him because they could not count on their own representatives or senators.

Islam teaches its followers that it is by the good works that one gets to go to heaven. Islam also teaches that God punishes those who commit bad deeds. It is no wonder that my dear father was so confused that he was being punished even though all his life he did good deeds by serving others. The good works doctrine seemed to have resulted in suffering with cancer instead of a peaceful reunion with God. Islam did not make sense to him or to the loved ones around him.

The elders told him that the flesh is of dust and is sinful and needed to be wasted away, and that suffering is good, for it is because of the suffering that we lose our sinful flesh.

I regret that no one was there to tell him that accepting God's gift for salvation, His Son, and humanity's only Savior is what he needed. By this time, about ten years into the Islamic Revolution, Christians were as scarce in Iran as aliens from Mars. Lost people could not give directions of the Way to another lost person. The blind could not lead another blind man. Islam failed my wonderful father.

My mother told me later that before he died, he went into a deep coma for three days. No food, drink, or medication was needed. He was in a deep, continuous sleep. Sometimes in my intimate moments with my Savior, I contemplate the possibility and even picture that during that period, the Lord reached out to him, he believed in Him, and "it was counted to him as righteousness" (Gen 15:6)!

My father was the rock of the family.

The plane that carried my father back home.
I never saw him again.

My mother will have an empty chair
next to her at family events.

My Mother—the Flower-Born

My mother's name in Farsi means "flower-born." My mother married my father when she was only fourteen years old. I always believed that my daughter Rebecca inherited her heart—one made out of gold! I believe that I learned my sacrificial love for my children and my granddaughter from her. She taught me how to give love and expect nothing in return. She taught me how to never worry whether people remembered my good deeds and service toward them or not, mainly because the only one whose opinion really counts does know and will remember!

I often tell my children and friends that my mother would make a great Christian. She never gossips; she never wishes ill for anyone, not even for her enemies. If anyone does her wrong, she prays that God would forgive that person. She always tries to please and help others and would never think negatively of people. In all certainty, her role model was not Prophet Mohammad!

Although she learned to read on her own, she never had any formal schooling. This always made her feel a little ashamed. It was after I came to know Christ and my whole outlook changed that I one day had an epiphany in my head. I realized why my mother was such a "Christian-like" woman. It was because she never went to school! Her mind did not get corrupted with Islam. She never had to read the Islamic verses that we read in school. She never had to repeat and memorize the verses that say, "God does not have a begotten and is not begotten" (Q: 19:88-92, Q: 112).

In the early years of the revolution when it was fashionable for women to go to Islamic studies, she didn't go because of her inability to read Qur'an, and thus, the "mal-training" did not take place. Her mind and heart stayed pure. She never had to write the word Allah. Although she could hear what the mullahs were saying, the words were not pictured in her mind and therefore would not leave a deep impression in her heart, mind, and soul.

We who went to school and learned the false theology found that unlearning it was an uphill road! Undoing the damage and releasing the strongholds were heavy labor that only the one whose burden is light can bear. My false theology was conquered with the help of the Lord. I was glad that I found the reason behind my mother's Christian-like character. That has given me hope that maybe God's grace will touch her too and her soul will be saved.

One memory I have of her is when I told her what my father said while he was here in the United States just months before he died. I told her that he told me, "I swear to God, there is no woman anywhere in the world like your mother!" She was glad to hear that after his death because in that culture, and that generation, husbands and wives always avoided these sentimental talks with each other. Even though my mother had never heard the words, "I love you" from her husband, she knew that he did love her and vice versa. She married him when she was a young fourteen-year-old and now for the first time she was alone. I cried just thinking about how lonely she must feel! Telling her what he had said brought a warm smile to her face. I saw how satisfying that was for her, as if all the hardships of the past forty-five or so years were worth it. I was glad to be an instrument in causing that satisfaction and inner joy in her.

During my father's battle with cancer, he sent one of his sons to the store to buy a beautiful eighteen-karat gold bracelet for my mother. He wanted to give it to her for their forty-fifth wedding anniversary. In his mind, after his death, if she ever needed money, she could sell that for a good amount of money. Of course during the past twenty years since he had passed on, she needed money many times, but she never could sell that bracelet because it was the last gift that he gave her. It was a sort of thank you from him for the hardship she endured during the battle with cancer, during the revolution and post-revolution years, during the eight years of war, and during the poverty years early in the marriage. She knew that he was appreciating her, and that meant the world to her. He loved her. That's what every wife would want to know about her husband.

One of the memories that I cherish in my heart about her is about a time when she was visiting me in the United States for the first time back in early 1990s. We went to visit an old family friend of ours. The discussion led to religion and then to Jesus. The friend's husband said how Jesus was better than Muhammad. My mother answered, "Well of course. He was the Son of God!"

This shocked me! Muslims do not believe that Jesus was the Son of God. But since the virgin birth of Jesus is also in the Qur'an, my mother used her own mind's logic and reasoning power (and a woman's child-bearing know-how) and concluded that He must be and would be the Son of God if the Spirit of God came upon Mary—a virgin—and she conceived! It made a perfect sense to her.

She is now in her mid-seventies and planning a trip to Mecca. She just wants to please God. I pray that someday soon she would come to know the Son of God personally and to experience the true inner joy and peace that surpasses all understanding.

2

GOD REALLY EXISTS!

The heavens declare the glory of God; the skies proclaim the work of his hands. Day after day, they pour forth speech; night after night they display knowledge.
—Psalm 19:1-3

The '70s were eventful years for me. The decade started with the glory of God being manifested in heavens, pouring out displays of love, truth, and knowledge, and it ended in uprooting of my country by the Islamic Revolution in 1979. I left the country I loved to go to an alien land where I found the true God and where I was delivered to His Kingdom.

It was a typical late summer evening in Ahwaz. The air was clean and cool. The sky was beautiful, deeply dark, and very inviting! The deep blue and silvery clouds were layered one on the top of the other and added to the depth of the space. My room was upstairs, away from a large noisy family of eleven, and had a balcony. We called it terrace. In the summertime, we slept on the terrace because it was cool. There were no central air conditioners back then, and if people had portable window types, they would run it only a few hours in the afternoon when temperature would reach up to 110 degrees. Every evening we would wash the terrace thoroughly and let it dry for about an hour. We would then spread out bedding and sleep under the stars.

The terrace of my room where the glory of God
filled the night sky.

Pol-e-Karoon in Ahwaz

The nights of Ahwaz were famous for their coolness and light breezes. Ahwaz was the heart of Khoozestan Province and the bedrock of the romantic *Karoon* River and its beautiful double-arc bridge, *Pole-Karoon*. I used to stare at the sunset over the river and admire the beauty and magnitude of God's creation. I could still picture the tall, majestic palm trees sweeping against each other and creating soothing background music for the passersby. People who didn't have terraces or upstairs at all would either sleep on their houses' roofs or in their front yards. The front yards were made of concrete and a part of the indoor.

I gazed into the infinite space with sparkling stars, a magnificent moon, and colorful, dynamic clouds dancing in the vastness of universe.

I was not a typical Persian girl. Growing up, I was a quiet, serious, yet very sensitive girl. I expressed my thoughts and feelings in my poems, compositions, and journal entries. I did not have many friends, and from a popularity standpoint, I was near zero or could not make anyone's list. For me, the culture did not have to dictate my beliefs. In other words, if one did not like a tradition, a belief, or a value system, I thought, it did not have to be a part of one's culture regardless of one's geographical upbringing. Moreover, since culture is a learned behavior, I believed any tradition-based behavior could also be unlearned! That is sometimes called going against the grain, but it was my opinion then that we were intelligent beings, able to think, rethink, and analyze. Just because something was a norm did not mean it should remain permanent.

But Iranian culture, inclusive of its national identity, politics, traditions, and religion, was one and the same. This was possible because we were not as diverse as were other parts of the world. Because of this inclusiveness and homogeneity of the people, I never had to face the challenges of being atypical—well, until I found the God of love! More on this later.

Being a Muslim was as much of an identity as was being a Persian. There was no difference or separation between the two. The two were woven tightly into one and were inseparable! The Western mind has much difficulty digesting and understanding this notion. One is born into Islam as one is born into Iranian identity, nationality, and the Persian race. Although we as Persians had a tremendous national and racial pride and generally thought of ourselves a "better" race than the Arabs, Islam, originally an Arab religion was (and still is) so ingrained into our identity that we stopped thinking and just believed in it. Questioning Islam was taboo, and it served no purpose. Belief in Islam was nonnegotiable!

We had a Qur'an in our home like every family, religious or nonreligious, had. It was stowed on the top shelf of our living room, collecting dust. It was there primarily to bring "good luck" or "God's favor" to the household. Growing up, I did not know anyone who read the Qur'an just to learn, understand, and God-forbid, to enjoy. Qur'an was read at weddings or funerals. Only a small percentage of people were mosque-goers, and selective passages were read there. During the shah's regime, it wasn't hip to be religious! Nowadays, in the Islamic Republic of Iran, it is hip only if one is religious. Today, being devoutly religious is to add to one's nationalism, accessibility, acceptability, and even good fortune.

The majority of Iranians had Qur'ans that were in the original Arabic language. Islamic leaders believed that the Qur'an must not be translated into any language because it could not be understood in any other language. Persians speak Farsi. We shared the alphabet and numbers with Arabic, but that was it. The challenge can be compared with Spanish for English speakers. Although an English speaker may easily read, "Como estas" (since the alphabet is the same as English), its meaning is known only to those who know the Spanish language.

This did not pose a problem since the intention of having the Qur'an generally was not to read it and follow it as a guideline in living but to protect the household from bad luck!

At the time, I did not agree with this reasoning (that the Qur'an can only be understood in Arabic) and thought instead that the reason was more about the incompetency of Arab scholars in learning other languages, such as English or French, and translating it. My current view on this is one other than these two theories. I believe the Qur'an's content was kept hidden for the sole purpose of keeping the people uninformed about its dangerous and violent nature, and about its uselessness and empty promises of afterlife, and more importantly, about its falsehood as being the Word of God.

Thus we, as Persians and Farsi speakers, had an added challenge in Islam. Although there were several Iranian Islamic scholars who spoke both languages, the few translated copies that were available were so poorly translated into Farsi that no one understood the text. People were expected to accept Qur'an as the Word of God (even if the Word could not be read or understood) and obey its power and message. I found out later that even Arabs had difficulty reading and understanding the Qur'an because of its meaningless use of words, confusion in topics presented, and lack of consistency and coherency in the messages. We dared not to think that Allah was a confused god, but the lack of meaning or profound revelation was our fault as imperfect human beings. We were expected to take it as the Word of God and to revere it without any questions or doubts. As good Muslims, we all did exactly that. More on this is provided in chapters 6 and 8.

Some people would open a Qur'an only during a crucial decision-making period in life. If they could read Arabic, they would read a verse or two. Most of the time they didn't know what it meant; they just trusted that whatever they read pleased Allah. People would open the Qur'an when they had a life issue or a decision to make and would read it to see if anything positive was there that would indicate that a good outcome or a negative word that would indicate a bad outcome, sort of like a fortune-telling exercise.

Most people who were seeking an answer to a question or issue would resort to reading just one word on the top of the page: good or bad. On top of each page in most Qur'an s was recorded either the word good or bad, and people who couldn't read Arabic (which were over 99 percent) would only read that word on top of the page and would either leave happy or disappointed. I did it myself. Later when I was able to read Arabic a little more and understood the meaning of the text, I found out that the selections of good and bad were all random! There was no correlation to the passages. It was meaningless. At the time, we did not think of this as superstitious. In the absence of an involved and caring God, this was perfectly reasonable. It was a natural Islamic thing to do.

People in Islam grow up believing that it is not necessary to understand the Qur'an. One just needs to believe in it as the Word of God because the religious leaders say so. Some who were mosque-goers would listen to the Mullahs reading it on Friday nights, and most would just weep and wail without ever understanding a word. Since the Arabic alphabet was the same as the Farsi alphabet (to a good extent), it was not too hard for us to read, but we did not know the meanings of words unless a deliberate attempt was made to learn them.

High schools had classes two hours a week in religion studies, in which we learned a little Arabic and a brief overview of the Qur'an and Islamic teachings. The teachings were not just out of the Qur'an. The Sharia contained the laws and moral standards written by the Prophet Mohammed and other Islamic scholars. Although we knew these were tied to our Islamic identity, we thought of them as the Arab's way of life. We were mentally separated from these laws and moral codes.

For example, there is a legal requirement of two women witnesses being equal to one man's witness, and the legal marriage age of nine for women was there in our Islamic heritage. But since the Islamic law did not rule Iran before the Revolution of 1979, these laws and regulations posed no threat to our way of life. They were not issues for discussion or debate among Muslim Iranians.

But for me, the atypical Persian girl, the truth was important. Although I was searching for the truth, I neither expected to find it within the boundaries of Islam, nor did I expect to find it outside the bounds of Islam. The latter wasn't a surprise, since anything outside Islam was so separate and irrelevant that we automatically did not think outside of the box.

But because of God's imprint on our hearts, regardless of how a society is purposefully and systematically isolated from outside world, we keep asking the same life-and-death questions. For example, what happens when I die? Where do we go when we die? Why am I here? Why does Islam say that it is a superior religion? Why is it the most complete revelation of God?

Since we were taught and programmed to think that Jews are not good and the Christians are "dirty" and *Kafar* (unbelievers) from a religious and moral sense, there was not much interest among people to find answers to these questions outside the framework of Islam. People in Iran were not encouraged to compare their belief system with other belief systems to see where they stood. Free will was a Western concept! (Of course, we had no idea that it was originally God's idea.)

Islam was embedded in our national identity. This caused most of the young people like myself to think that there is an intrinsic difference and separation between the Easterners and the Westerners and there is no point trying to bridge the gap. But my young mind was convinced that this is not what God wants from us, if indeed there is only one God. If Islam's Allah is the God of Christians and Jews, then we are connected not by choice but by natural and supernatural laws beyond our control and regardless of what Islamic leaders would like. That fact makes the separation illogical.

To look at it from another point of view, it meant that since Muslims were self-proclaimed enemies of the Christian and Jews, it is very possible and likely that Allah is not the God of Jews and Christians; otherwise he would not allow this animosity. Indeed, even from a young age living in Iran, I knew that Muslims did not like Christians and Jews. In later years and even now, when speaking to so-called educated Muslims, they may tell you, "We are not enemies of the people, just their governments!" This is absurd and untrue.

Looking at this question from the other side of this coin, if Christians and Jews are so close, so supportive of each other, and so entwined with each other, could it be because they have in common the same God?

To summarize my thoughts as a inquisitive teenager, I believed that if we proclaimed to be one of the three monotheistic religions, meaning believing in one God, by definition that meant the same God, and therefore Islam should not be hateful and isolated from the other two and its doctrine should not be opposed to the other two religions. In fact, it should be in harmony with them, even if it claimed to be more "complete."

I was a logical person too. I needed things to make sense. Logical thinking and scientific reasoning were extremely impressive and popular in the '60s and the '70s in Iran. In my opinion, these two decades (minus 1979) were the mini-enlightenment age in Iran. The country was progressive in almost all areas, from women's rights and fashion to arts and sports to science and technology. But one area was off the table of debate or change: religion. Since I did believe in *Khoda* (Farsi for God), even if in an abstract way, I logically accepted the no-questions-asked policy!

During the month of Ramadan, I fasted from dawn to dusk and prayed the ritual prayers as I was taught. "Good" girls fasted; parents were always proud of the children who fasted. During dawn and evening prayers, I always would end my ritual with an, *"O God please set me on the right path"* in my own language. This was always my wish. I didn't understand much of what I was saying in Arabic, but this I knew I wanted. One of the few lines in Arabic I understood, *"Lam yalad va lam yoolad,"* which means, "Allah does not have a child and is not a child of anyone" (Q: 112). Since this line was rhythmic, it was easy to memorize it in Arabic; thus the Islamic doctrine that God does not have a son made the Christian doctrine that said Jesus is the Son of God ridiculous. That idea was settled and closed in our minds.

With all the love and morality-based upbringing we had at home, the religious rituals that were indicative of being the good Muslim girl, with all of the scientific, logical, and intellectual mind that I was labeled to have, and with a rare philosophical yet romantic approach to life, I was still empty inside—miserably empty.

I also knew what I was empty of: love. I craved love but not the sorts of love people were talking about. I was empty of God's love. My heart was aching for an answer! I often felt I was boxed in, like a prisoner. I used to look at the sky and wish to break the barriers, leave the box, and find out what else was out there. This was unlike girls my age in Iran who only wished for a good romance and a happy marriage after high school. That, for me, was the death of everything.

I needed to know who I was, what the purpose of my life on earth was, and what this life meant. I took refuge in books. I read over fifty books in just one summer! I don't recall any of them were religious. We knew a few categories of books were banned, but I was too young to know what or why. I knew books critical of the Shah were banned, but that seemed normal to us. What I didn't know at the time was some books on Christianity were banned also, but since we were Muslim, it wasn't a big deal. I read secular books, mostly life-related or about philosophy or biographies of famous historical people.

Although I seemed very confident (a bit to the arrogant side,) very secure, and kind of a know-it-all to outsiders, inside I longed for a deeper, truer meaning of life. I wanted to be loved in a deeper, more meaningful way, and I wanted to know my Creator. I wanted to know who the Creator was and why He created us!

I was a hopeless romantic too. I liked to express myself skillfully using the rich Persian language. I loved painting portraits and landscapes and was determined to tell the world of my longing. I also loved reading and writing poems.

I recently read a poem of mine that was written when I was sixteen or so. My younger sister discovered it in our home in Iran and brought it with her when she came to the United States in 2002. The writing was of a good quality that would be difficult for me to write now, but what amazed me were the content and the inspirational cry shown in the poem. It was all about calling nature—the mountains, the oceans, the birds, and the plants—to bow down and worship the Great Creator, for, the poem said, *"He is the only one worthy of the worship!"* I, as a Christian now, was impressed about the fact that my mind and soul were filled with the need to worship the true God, although I had no personal knowledge of Him!

The world as a whole was a big question mark and an unknown place to me, but I was aware of its existence and knew I lacked the knowledge of knowing it. There were no computers or Internet back then. There were no instant images of other countries, people, or information. Books were the only gateways to knowledge of physical places beyond one's residence.

America in particular was like another planet to us. It had strange people with strange ideas and very beautiful skins, but still it was like a dream—a fairytale. I read the books of Jack London and Pearl S. Buck and listened to European icons such as Beethoven and Chopin to connect with my external world. America had invented television, and that was the most amazing thing for us! It was a symbol of luxury and wealth. We had one, and I mostly loved the old movies that showed nuns in convents. I was impressed with how their lives were completely committed to God and service to others. They were spared from experiencing the corruption of open societies.

I told my father once, "I know what I would like to be when I grow up." He laughed and asked, "What?" I said, "A nun." He laughed even more and said, "That's impossible because there is no such thing as nun in Islam!" and so I never thought about it anymore.

On that particular evening, I was lying down in my terrace and gazing with nostalgia at the beautiful sky with a luminous, silvery moon, twinkling stars, and colorful layers of clouds. I say nostalgia because I always felt that I belonged to another place! I always felt that I wasn't really complete as I was where I was. I sometimes blamed my longing on Iran and its limitations; other times I blamed it on Islam and its restrictions and view toward women.

I surveyed the mysterious yet welcoming sky from the left to the right. I always knew there was a Great Creator behind this beautiful nature, but that is all I knew. I wanted to know who I was in reference to the world around me. I wanted so much to know if people's lives mattered and if someone was aware of each one of us no matter from what part of the planet we may be.

We, in Islam, believed that God was somewhere far, far away from us, detached from His creation and unconcerned about the everyday lives of people. I remember that when people spoke of something they hope for, they would say, *"Insha-allah,"* which means, "Allah willing," but it was always said in the context of hopeless situations. In other words, "Allah willing" was a closing statement for when a person's only certainty was his uncertainty about the outcome and he wanted to end a conversation! I could now see how hopeless we were!

As a matter of fact, God was so far, distant, and detached from us that we never used a pronoun such as He or Him for God. We were told that God is spirit and personal pronouns such as He or She were not fitting because they would "lower" Him to our level. God was too different, too impersonal, and therefore, unknowable. We were not taught that we were made in His image! With that precept, there was no reason to ever believe that we could *know* our Creator.

So that night, lost in the beauty of the sky and the stars above, I murmured, "Oh God, where are You? Who are You? I want to know You." These words came from the deepest core of my soul. There was no expectation for any answer, no expectation of anyone to hear me. I was only uttering these words to calm my inner longing.

I always wanted to know who I was in relation to the world around me. I was curious about why I was here on this earth and what my purpose was in life, but I never thought it was possible to ever find out the answer to those questions. After all, many scholars, philosophers, and artists for centuries asked these questions. I was only a young seventeen-year-old girl from a small town of a small, unknown country with no education, wealth, or position, either of myself or of my family, so why would I have any hope in getting answers? That was why most people didn't ask these questions. They were simple words and short sentences, but they were unanswerable questions.

Quickly my thoughts moved on, and for just an instant, I forgot the deep cry of my soul of moments ago. Few seconds later, I looked back at the sky, and said, "Oh, my God!" I saw a sight out of this world! I saw a beautiful heart perfectly carved out of clouds and placed in front of the moon. The edges of the heart were perfectly drawn, as if the heart was not made out clouds, but it seemed like it was drawn with the finest pen and with extreme precision. I had not seen a heart that beautiful and that perfectly drawn before!

No one can describe a perfect shape for a heart, but that heart, I knew, was perfect! The bright rays of the hidden moon stretched from all sides of the heart so anyone could have looked up at that moment and seen it shine. What a glorious sight it was, although the word was not in my vocabulary then. The perfect beauty of this heart is all I could think about, even to this day.

God used His sky as a canvas to draw me to His heart and to present it to me. Tears of belief poured down my cheeks. I hardly heard those few words that I murmured myself. How did God hear me? He was there next to me in that balcony to hear me uttering those few words, yet He was also up there, millions of miles away, in the vastness of the universe to answer me! *God really exists!* I thought with awe. He used His universe to display His love and His power to me!

It would be decades later that I read in the Bible: "The heavens declare the glory of God . . . night after night, they display knowledge" (Ps. 19:1-3), and I would recall this night.

For the first time, I personally felt God's presence! For the first time, I knew with certainty that God exists. The knowledge was given to me, and He used the most effective tool a teenager, especially a romantic one, would understand: He drew me His heart!

Philosophically, this personal experience was a breakthrough. It proved God really exists! God is real! All the books and Islamic studies in schools, conversations, speeches, visits to shrines, and fasting rituals were secondhand information that I, and millions of others, had taken for truth and believed. They were ideas and facts I had accepted; tasks I had performed. But this was different. God is real, true, and active! Not only did this vision prove that God existed and is real, but it also proved that He is good! He is so good that He did not ignore me for being too little, too insignificant, a girl, and practically a nobody. He was so good that He cared and paid attention to my questions, and finally, the best conclusion, He was so good that He gave me His heart! And as any teenager would testify, that meant He loved me!

I was still crying! However, these tears were no ordinary tears. They were tears of a special joy—a joy I had never experienced before. They were tears of belief, tears of discovery, and tears of solving the mystery of an unknowable God! I remember the overwhelming feeling I had then. The Creator of the universe took time to converse with me! The more I became aware of how supernatural and wonderful this experience was, the more I became aware of how special, in God's eyes, I was. And the more I became aware of how special, in God's eyes, I was, the more knowable and accessible He became in my eyes.

God came as close to me as to tell me He loved me by giving me His heart. This was a breakthrough! This was beyond Islam! You see, in Islam, God was characterized mostly by His power, especially power of judgment and punishment, but never by love and tenderness. Fear is the centerpiece of Islam. The Muslims' loyalty to the faith and allegiance to Allah and its prophet was tied to this centerpiece: fear. It was not the kind of fear that

I came to read about and understand in my Christian walk, which has the meaning of awe-inspiring, adoration, and respect, but fear as in fear of someone who is going to kill or destroy; fear of a vengeful, dictatorial, merciless, heartless ruler. Yes, Muslims would call Him merciful, but that also has its roots in the judgment characteristic. We, in Islam, never would say, "God is love," yet He showed me that He was indeed love! More specifically, He loved even the little, insignificant me!

My life was never the same again. I had but a taste of God's love, and I wanted, so desperately, the full course! Now I knew, personally, that God knew who I was, where I was, and what was in my mind. I knew that He has made me and put me on this planet for a purpose. If I only knew His Word then, "'For I know the plans I have for you,' declares the LORD, 'plans to prosper you and not to harm you'" (Jer. 29:11).

Now I had a burning desire to find Him. Although I was blown away by His overwhelming display of love, my young mind was still working and thinking. I knew with certainty that I could not find God in Iran! Iran was devoid of God's love. Iran was devoid of God's knowledge. That was my experience and my belief. That night I pledged to find Him even if I had to go to the ends of the earth!

I kept this sacred vision that turned my heart and my world upside down all to myself. It was such an out of this world experience that not only would people not have believed me, but I believed that they would never understand. I also knew I wouldn't be able to adequately and fully explain its beauty, its profoundness, and its truth.

Islam had no miracles. Mohammed did not perform any miracles like Moses or Abraham or Jesus (*Isa*). No one speaks or hears Allah! No one has a relationship with Allah, so I kept this personal experience to myself. It was a fabulous secret that was too sacred and unbelievable for the people around me. I was afraid that if I told them, they would fail to see profoundness, its eternal nature, and its love that was not like any love we knew on earth. I was afraid that people would discard the vision as my imagination, maybe randomness of clouds, or even a lie to get attention. I preferred to keep the sweetness of His love to myself because I did not see anyone who was ready to receive it. I knew the true God connected with me, and that alone was nothing short of miracle.

3

REVOLUTIONS— SMALL AND BIG

Yet when I hoped for good, evil came; when I looked for light, then came darkness.

—Job 30:26

During the shah's reign, the country prided itself in having experienced the White Revolution. It was called white because no bloodshed occurred. The revolution constituted of a drastic national development and reform program that included land reforms, political reforms, and social reforms. These changes occurred in less than three years between 1960 and 1963 and changed the life of Iran from an agricultural country, mostly under the control or influence of foreign governments, to an independent, rich, and progressive country. The point that underscored this revolution was that no blood had been shed. It was one of the shah's most treasured achievements.

The country had not experienced the Islamic revolution yet, so people used the word revolution in its most positive and light sentiment, such as a revival or a change. That was about to change. Life was about to teach us the true meaning of revolution, and life, as we knew it was about to change both at a personal level and at the national level.

I graduated from my high school in 1972, and since my sister, Pari, was already married, my father put all his hopes in me to go to college. All his other children were younger than me. He worked very hard all his life, and all he wanted was for his children to be well educated and to get good jobs and high positions in government or private industry. He especially was optimistic about my future and knew that I would be successful because I loved reading and learning, and had an inquisitive and logical mind. It also appeared to him and others that I was not marriage material. So when I was accepted in a college in Isfahan, he and the rest of the family were ecstatic. My mother later told me that the news of my going to college "exploded like a bomb" in Ahwaz and MIS! It was a private college and therefore, very expensive. I heard years later that my father sold one of our Persian carpets to pay for my tuition! He always kept a big smile for us, so we never knew if he were hurting financially.

During the '60s and '70s, Tehran's women went through the American feminism phase. They started to wear miniskirts and the latest fashion, makeup, etc. They even picked up smoking as the sign of gender freedom. They learned about the latest marital issues of the American movie stars and knew the latest Beatles and pop songs. The disco clubs were very popular, and I believe the country was experiencing a social revolution by the end of the '60s and early '70s. America was their role model, and freedom was defined as doing what women didn't used to do in Iran. Men learned to be gentlemen! They respected women, especially the educated ones. The secularity of the society was now an indicator of its progress and higher civilization. Religion was only for small towns and uneducated people. The signs of this social revolution were mostly concentrated in the nation's capital.

Iran is a paternal society. Men are always taken more seriously than women. If there were a girl living alone or even going shopping alone, people would not respect her as much as if she were accompanied with her father, a brother, or a close male relative. Men were thought of as predators, and families' priorities were always to protect the girls. Even a rumor of a man befriending one's daughter was a disgrace to the family. Every good girl's effort was that she would not be labeled with another man before her marriage.

Good girls didn't have boyfriends, so if a girl liked someone, she would keep it to herself and guard the information with her life! For men, though, it was exactly the opposite. A young man, who had a girlfriend, whether secretly or openly, was admired! It demonstrated his maturity, his likability, and his readiness to think about family, etc. It was a sort of conquering satisfaction, and it conveyed a message of manhood that nothing else would.

I soon found out that my new home in Isfahan was a religious town! I had to wear *"chador"* to go to the public bath—only a couple of blocks from where I lived. The women were more critical, accusatory, and ready to label young girls.

Although there were a lot of rental apartments and houses, it was not appropriate for a young girl to rent a place for herself and live on her own. One reason was the lack of safety and security. Western countries, especially America, were regarded as a symbol of immorality, crime, and other social misconduct. We were told it was because they were not Muslims. But soon I realized the reasons behind why Iranian parents keep their daughters on such a close watch; it was because of what may happen if someone finds out a young woman is living alone. They were afraid of their own men!

In my few years of living in Isfahan, I found out that most of what was preached about Iran and Iranians in regard to morality, hospitality, and kindness were only external and for show, and reality was something totally different. Integrity, honesty, and genuine love of neighbor were as rare as a flying carpet!

The women of Isfahan were their own worst enemy. They often would start labeling or spreading rumors about a neighbor's girl and spread lies. Parents and even young women did everything they could to avoid this, because it was an honor thing and because the girl may become unmarryable! I hated these ridiculous cause and effect things, but as long as I was a part of Iran, I was involved as well as affected, if only by association!

A year later, my father rented a house and sent my younger brother to Isfahan so we could be together and protect each other. This house had its own bath, and I did not need to go to a public bath. This was a small freedom from the watchful Isfahani women, but I still had to deal with their constant watch from their windows, front doors, etc.

My brother, Bahman, was the apple of my eye! He was a true gentleman in a world infested with arrogance, selfishness, and corruption. He inherited my father's leadership, passion for serving, and competence, and my mother's wit and sweetness of spirit, blended with his own unique attributes of artistic talents (he was a calligrapher) and cheerfulness of heart.

One of my memories from the time we lived together in Isfahan is about a time when he was down with a severe case of flu. I was so worried, mostly because I didn't know how I could help him to get better. I called my parents and told them, and my father sent a friend of his who lived nearby to come and check on my brother. He came and visited us then called my father back and told him, "Your son is OK, but I am not so sure about your daughter!"

At this writing, he is in the hospital and very sick. He has been diagnosed with stomach cancer. I miss him dearly! My most fervent prayer is that the Lord would draw him near and that he would come to know his true God and Savior! My entire church family is praying for him.

In my few years in Isfahan away from my father's home, I learned a lot about life. I went to school in the mornings and worked part time in the afternoon. Most of my learning and growing up took place at my work environment. I worked in a four-star hotel. I quickly found out that my father's love for his daughters and his treatment of my mother and other women was unique and not shared by the greater culture of our country. It was at my workplace that I realized men were predators! In their speech or deeds, it was apparent that they had very little respect for women. Women were like objects for them. We didn't have the labor laws such as gender discrimination, sexual harassment, or a code of conduct in regard to acts that made it a hostile working environment. Most of the times what men said, felt, or believed had precedence over what a woman employee said.

Based on all my observations in regard to the role, treatment, and state of men and women in Iran, I concluded that everything that is determined as bad for women is good for men, and everything that is bad for men (which is not many) is also bad for women! Women seemed to lose no matter what.

Everyone in our family and extended family and friends knew that I had a different, sort of rebellious personality. I did not think that having many marriage prospects was indicative of a woman's value. I did not believe that men were smarter or better or in any way had more inalienable rights than women. I was aware of women's cultural limitations and knew that even after graduation from college, my chances of getting a good job and excelling in my career are very few, but I also knew that I did not wish to be a man since I believed the world needed the tenderness and the compassion of women no matter where they are. It was in Isfahan when I realized that the Iran box was too tight for easy breathing, and I needed to extend my wings to the outside of the box.

One sunny afternoon, I was walking in downtown Isfahan. I gazed at the population passing me by, mostly men. An overwhelming sense of fear and displeasure overtook me, and I thought, *one of these men would someday be my husband!* The thought went into my brain and then into my soul and caused a deep, aching pain within. My heart ached even from the passing thought. I could even picture my life meaninglessly passing me by before I would live it. Life without meaning was not what I wanted. Having a husband and children seemed like a dead end. I must add here that since I did not know my Lord then, life and marriage and children did not have that heaven tie that it does now.

Having a husband and a bunch of children was like going through life systematically, checking a box. The pleasure part was shopping, schools, and a wedding and then repeating it all over again. There was nothing beyond ourselves that we were living for. There was no permanent impact I could make to this life on earth. I would be like an ant with my head down, taking food from one point to another point and not being aware of what happens on top of me or on the sides of me. The reality would be a small, limited, and finite reality. I tried not to think about it. When the hopelessness overshadowed my common sense that day, I suddenly remembered my God who gave me His heart a year before, and I knew, now for sure, that He knows where I am and what my heart's desires are. I knew that He also knew what were *not* my heart's desires.

I was two years into the college and living in Isfahan. I majored in statistics—a man's territory in academia in Iran. Although those who knew me believed I was very smart, I knew better. Intellectually, I was just an average. I remembered my father was so proud of me because I was the first in the family to go to college!

Even though my father wanted me to concentrate on school, I felt, as an adult, a little ashamed of asking him for money for daily expenses, so I found a job in a four-star hotel in town. This hotel was one of the two top hotels mostly occupied by long-term foreign guests. It was my first job ever.

I learned so much about my own people during the few months I worked there. All my life I was shielded from people at large, especially from the opposite sex. I thought every man was like my father and every woman was like my mother! I was totally wrong. I couldn't imagine having a deliberate agenda in mind to hurt others or to use others. I didn't know women purposely flirted with men at work! Moreover, I did not know it was considered a part of women's equality.

In my first year at work, a nice Italian man came to my office area and asked me to type a few papers for him. This, he knew, was above and beyond the regular hotel services. It was a five-minute typing job, and he gave me a bill equivalent to twenty dollars today. The coworker who sat near me told me that I should give some of the money to him and also to the other person who worked in the office. I said no. He said, "Well, I am going to report this to the higher manager because it is stealing!"

The manager came and asked me about it. I told him exactly how the twenty dollars came to me. He said it is not stealing, but since I used the hotel's typewriter, then the money should go into hotel's account. I said it would be fine with me. The coworker who wanted some of the money smirked as if he had won, but of course he lost because nothing went to him and his accusation was rejected also. But he was deeply gratified that no money went to me.

The next time that same Italian man came along to ask me to type something for him, I wrote a little note in English that said, "Do not pay me anything because it will not go to me." He understood. When he left without paying, the same coworker asked, "He didn't pay?" I said no. He said, "Well, we'll see about that." He went to the manager again and told on the Italian man! I found out whatever money they asked him to pay went to the hotel's account again. He never came back!

I learned a lot from that. I learned that my countrymen were so greedy, so hungry for money, that they would stoop so low as to deprive a college student—a young girl—from having a few dollars if it were not shared with them. I also found out that my countrymen were so comfortable to pin labels on to people if it served them and seemed to not have any sense of right and wrong. I realized that although they displayed an image of graciousness to foreigners, they spoke badly about them after any contact and even wished them ill. I heard a lot of gossiping about how Americans are rich and spoiled and how my countrymen wished them "hell."

These men were nothing like my father. My father had a heart that was selfless and beat for the poor, for the disadvantaged, and for the lowly. His mind was an open mind, a visionary. He was unique, and so he instilled in his children the idea of thinking out of the box.

There was a lady in her mid-forties who worked in that office in the hotel. She used to laugh and joke with the men in the office a lot. Although I did not fully understand what was going on, I did not feel comfortable hearing some of her comments. She would hold one of the men's arms and drag him to the manager's office and would say to others, "Don't knock; we want to be alone," and would laugh out loud continuously. When I made a comment to one of the coworkers, he looked at me as if I had come from a different planet and said, "Look, this woman is a *beautiful* woman who works in a *hotel!*" He emphasized the words "beautiful" and "hotel."

I learned later that, generally, women who worked in hotels had a bad image. He stressed the word beautiful, which caused me to think he meant something other than beautiful. That's when I found out not all women were like my mother.

I had a lot to learn about people. This was the first time I detected the lack of integrity among my countrymen. This was only a few years after my vision in the sky when God manifested His power and love to me, and although I never talked to anyone about it because it was so sacred, so special, and so unbelievable, its impact was all too visible in my thinking and attitude in life. I knew money, power, or politics are never a sound foundation for building a life worthy of human beings. I knew that a higher, more glorious level of reality exists that makes all the world's wealth equal to dirt! I was aware of this higher reality of God, and although its depiction was, at best, an abstract in my mind, I knew I was going to find it and be a part of it! I knew that love played a big role in God's reality. That was something that was lacking in my country between people. People are hospitable, yes, but right after one leaves their home, they talk bad about the guests behind their backs. Sometimes even the interactions between family members and extended family was less than genuine.

I never liked things from the surface perspective. I liked to see the depth before I attached any quality to anything. True unconditional love was rare or nonexistent in my country; my parents, though, were exceptional in having shown true love to their children and to the people around them.

The *chadori* women in Isfahan were all religious, but God didn't seem to have a role in their daily living. Selfishness, resentment, envy, jealousy, lies, and deceptions were pervasive. When I shared my outlook with others, people thought I was too critical and too unrealistic and that my observations were pessimistic and unmerited. They thought I was unfairly judgmental. I was not believed often. I was accused of being too emotional about life—too sensitive, too serious, and too idealistic.

But I was certain that my now-personal God agreed with me. I had a smile within my heart! *He,* I thought, *understands what I mean about the lack of true love!*

My Small Revolution

At the hotel where I was working, there was an American guest who used to come and stop by our office area just to chat. He was a middle-aged man who had a German accent. Later he stated that he was a German-American Jew who worked for an American contractor that was helping Iran to get its helicopter-manufacturing plant off the ground in support of the Royal Air Force. He was intrigued by my curiosity and my education, so he came to chat more often. This was the very first American I ever met. I was very curious to know how Americans thought, behaved, and treated others. All we knew of Americans was through television. The Hollywood movies and television shows like *Little House* were popular. We thought of Americans as superior in race, intelligence, and knowledge. This was years before the Internet age, and so America was still an exotic, wonderful mystery to us.

I don't know why he stressed his Jewishness. In pre-revolution Iran, being a Jew was not much of a stigma, but it wasn't something to brag about either. Although people did not like Jews, the dislike was not so intense as to cause segregation, unemployment, harassment, or any mistreatment like in today's Iran. The integration of Jews into the society had strong and ancient roots. The American business motto that says, "Leadership begins at the top" is a good practice. The shah did not compartmentalize the country by different treatments or advocating different treatments of different groups in Iran. In fact, he acknowledged and appreciated the contribution of different groups of Iranians to the service of the country. Jews were not hidden and did not shy away from the public. They were as comfortable as Christian and Muslim Iranians.

As an inexperienced young woman just coming into a larger society, I did not know the issues involved in interfaith or internationality marriages until this middle-aged man proposed to me. It was only thirteen days after we met! We had a few breakfasts and dinners together. During these dates, I learned that the difference between how Americans thought about romantic relationships and how Iranians thought of them were as vast as space and as far as my imagination could tolerate!

I was still in a sudden cultural shock myself when I told my parents of my plans to marry this American. My parents, especially my father, were absolutely opposed to it, first, because he was many years my senior; second, because he was not a Muslim; third, because he was a Jew; and fourth, because he was a foreigner, which meant my father couldn't check him out.

My father wanted to know who this man was. He wanted to protect me from "foreigners who come to Iran to deceive and steal women." This accusation was a typical one in pre-revolutionary Iran. The phrase "who he was" had a different interpretation depending who asks; for an American it means, "What is his name?" But for an Iranian father, it means who are his parents, where are they from—that is what country, what tribe, what group—what is his job, his education, his background, his honesty, etc.

My relationship with my family soured and then was severed for a long time. The loss of the precious relationship I had with my father broke my heart the most.

I married this German-American Jew who was twenty-nine years my senior on October 23, 1975, and my small *revolution* exploded like a bomb in my hometown, this time it was more like a dirty bomb! When the time came for us to be at the office of a cleric to make it legal and final, my father came to serve as a witness just to protect my honor! Women in Iran are honored by the weight of their men kin. If a woman has no father, brother, or uncle, she has very little worth in the eyes of people. My father swallowed his pride and his principles for me. I knew that was true love.

I will never know how much this revolutionary act and my follow-up of leaving the country contributed to my father's development of colon cancer, but my mother and other family members told me that he was never the same after that. He was disappointed and brokenhearted. No one has ever done such a thing as this in our Bakhtiari background. My father was a very prominent and respected man and a leader in my hometown and in our extended family circle. This was an unspeakable act. To top it off, there was no wedding of any sort. This was even more of a disgrace for my family. My rebellious nature finally bore fruit, and the fruit was not sweet. It brought sadness, grief, and shame to my family, of which I am forever remorseful.

The marriage was anything but "two become one flesh." (Gen 2:24.) We were as different as Mars and Venus. With my family angry with me, having lost my friends and my school, I felt very cornered and isolated. Even with my little life experience, I knew that my husband must have had a very troubling childhood. Besides, he had just come from Vietnam, and the experience of war was too fresh for him. For me, it just meant that I had made my bed, and I needed to sleep in it. I knew divorce was impossible in Iran. Even suicide was better than divorce in those days, especially in respected families such as mine. The scandal would have been unimaginable, so I made a decision to live with my self-made revolution and try to make the best of it.

I recall a night when I almost died as the result of my husband's jealousy. We were watching television when my favorite singer, Vigen, started to sing. I was excited and told him that Vigen was my all-time favorite singer. All of a sudden, he got very angry. He pulled me forward toward the television, as I struggled to stay put, and said, "Kiss him, kiss him if you like him." I was stunned at his reaction. I thought to myself, *don't people in America like male singers?* I recalled various foreign entertainers, such as Elvis Presley, Tom Jones, and Engelbert Humperdinck, who were famous and popular singers, and then there were many American actors. I didn't understand why liking a singer was such a big deal to my husband.

The rage, jealousy, and distrust were so new to me. I had never seen a person like that before. A few minutes after that, I went through a very strange shock. I fell to the floor and started to feel injected by thousands of upright, sharp needles. It was as though the needles were orderly grouped and stood upright under me, from my head to my toe. I could feel my entire body being pierced by the needles' tips. I tried to hold my body above the sharp tips, but I was not able to help myself, yet I tried to move to my right, then to my belly, then to my back, and finally to my left, but there was no escape. I was terrified of my weight falling flat on the sharp needles! Death, I knew, was coming quickly and was about to swallow me! As I felt my body fall on the thousands of upright big needles, I lost consciousness.

I believed with all certainty that I was dying and had no memory of how and when the experience ended till the next day when my husband brought it up. He said, "You were calling on God the whole night." Then I remembered how I was near death. I remembered the thousands of sharp needles piercing into my body and the agonizing time when I was unconscious or unaware of my body convulsion.

And now I knew why I was awake and alive. He saved me. The God of love saved me—the one who painted the sky and gave me His precious heart just a few years before! He was real to me, not an abstract being any longer. He existed, and He loved me. Even during the shock and unconsciousness, without using my brain or will, from the core of my being I had called on Him.

Years later when I told this to a friend of mine who is a registered nurse, she told me it was seizure. She said in some rare cases, when a person experiences extreme trauma, especially emotional or psychological, the brain and body go through shock or seizure and it leads to person losing awareness or consciousness. I still remember the image of lying on top of a bed of sharp upright needles, and I thank my Lord for saving me.

A year after our marriage, I was with a child. Like any young bride, I was looking forward to telling my husband that we were going to have a child. When he came from work and I told him, he threw out what was in his hands and shouted some nonsense words at me. He definitely did not share my joy of expecting our first child. He threw one of his biggest fits, spit out some of his worst vocabulary, and asked me to have an abortion.

This event was the saddest, most traumatic of all for me. I was trapped in a bad marriage, isolated from all family and friends, and very inexperienced and scared. I gave in. He arranged it in an American clinic in Isfahan, and I went there to end the growth of my first child. I was alone during the whole time. The dreams of killing my own child haunted me for years. The memory of the vision of God's heart was hidden in my heart and in my mind, but my grief did not have a God-perspective. I know the abortion would have not happened if I knew my Savior then.

My grief was just at the human level—a mother losing a child, and losing it as the result of her own act. After a few years, I decided to put the memory behind me. I did not tell a soul, not even my mother or my sisters, about it. I kept everything to myself. I never spoke to my husband about my pains, my disappointments, and my sadness, because he was the source of them all,

Although I knew God was aware of my situation, I was, at times, disillusioned at why I ended up with someone who seemed to be my enemy. As a Muslim, I believed I didn't deserve to have a bad marriage since I was a good person. I wasn't sure why I was being punished. Years later, I found out the answer to my "whys". God used a Jew—His special possession (Ex. 19:5), to pluck me out of the upcoming revolution where not only it became a killing field for many, but also 'cleansed' Iran from Christians and Jews by murdering them, particularly those who would be turning away from Islam. God of love who always goes ahead of us, made sure that my eternity with Him is sealed. What men of darkness meant for evil, God used for good. (Gen. 50:20).

Brokenhearted, dead-spirited, and heavy-burdened with guilt, sadness, and shame, I took refuge in the peaceful sky every night. I wrote poems of despair and longing. I was in great need of a Deliverer, and although my eyes were still closed to the ultimate truth and I could not claim any intellectual expertise in any area and my small two-person family was not even close to a successful happy home, somehow I knew that I would be delivered from my prison, which was my life.

The political climate began to change toward more turbulence and uncertainty, and the sandy grounds of Iran began to shake as I had never imagined before. Darkness was about to become the law of the land!

My Country's Big Revolution

The year 1978 marked the beginning of the national Islamic Revolution. I had never seen my country in such a volatile state before! There were demonstrations for and against the shah day and night. A military curfew was in place, and soldiers with machine guns were at every corner and intersection, both day and night. I was too shocked to know what was happening.

People were on the edge, ready to explode with smallest conversation, and no one trusted anyone. People wanted freedom. The monarchy had stripped them of any form of freedom of speech, freedom of expression, or freedom to elect their government lawmakers.

There were stories of strikes, demonstrations, deaths and injuries, and imprisonments everywhere. Various strikes caused a scarcity of food, goods, and electricity. The country's heart was being ripped apart from inside out, and we all knew the worst was coming at a faster pace. The streets at night smelled of fear and blood and had whispers of the coming bloodshed and deaths.

Americans seemed to have seen these types of changes before because they predicted the conditions of the coming days very accurately. Iranians, however, were all confused, scared, and very agitated. All they wanted was to bring the shah down. They believed that anyone, any system, or any regime would be better and less oppressive than what they had. The Muslim cleric Ayatollah Khomeini promised all that the people lacked—justice, equality, peace, and happiness through Islam—but I don't believe anyone knew what an Islamic Republic really was! All the focus was on toppling the shah.

The shah and his family left the country on January 16, and so Americans and other foreigners were forced to evacuate. I called home. My sister answered, and I told her that I was on my way to the Tehran airport and would be leaving the country that day. I told her to give the message to my parents.

I left my country on January 29, 1979, a day before Ayatollah Khomeini landed in Iran! Although the thought of marrying my fellow Iranian men disturbed me and brought a strange fear in me a few years before, I felt extremely sorry and sad for my country and for its people, even for the men.

I saw the faces of 60 million sheep without a shepherd! But that was just a tip of the iceberg. Those who marched in the streets and gave their lives for the revolution had no idea what they were getting instead. Iran was about to plunge deeper into an even darker reality.

As I, and many others, walked to catch our planes out of the country, the spirit of fear filled the air and passed by us. I could even smell it. I was not a devout Muslim or anything close to a scholarly expert, but I knew what Islam had done to Arabs and Africans elsewhere. I knew enough to know that this was not a cure for Persians' problem. Most people thought that Khomeini, being an Iranian himself, would be different than, say, the rulers of Saudi Arabia and so he would bring peace and justice and eliminate the immoralities the Westerners had brought to Iran. They thought he would establish Islamic Utopia—envy for the world, including the Arab world.

There is a saying that knowledge is the key to power, so the lack of knowledge is the reason for the lack of power. People in Iran had no knowledge of the Qur'an and its teachings. We were Persians, and the language was Farsi. More than 98 percent of Iranians didn't know what was written in the Qur'an. In contrast, nearly 98 percent of all adults knew Hafez's poetry from heart!

Only the Qur'an's prayer verses and some fundamental principles were taught in schools. People did not know the origins and the bloody history of Islam, the spirit of death it was controlled by, and the goals and objectives of this spirit. But Khomeini knew. He was a well-known scholar in Islamic studies. He knew exactly what would become of our precious Iran in the near future.

Finally the new regime came under the protective umbrella of the prince of this world. Just as fourteen hundred years ago he used the political ambitions, strong will, and determination of one man—Mohammed—to bring a sea of lost souls to himself, now he used the political ambitions of another man, Ayatollah Khomeini, who interestingly claims to be a direct descendent of Mohammad, to plunge the nation into a bottomless pit, all for one purpose and one purpose only: to steal, destroy, and kill.

I later wrote this few lines of poem:

> Woe to a nation who bore children
> And later forsook them
> Who saw the soiled plates of food
> And did not wash them

Woe to those who sold their brothers and neighbors
For the pleasure of being the devil's slave
Those who sold their souls for a day of favor
And left begging for another, the next day

Woe to those who are the most merciless
Who killed and ate and ruled.

I left my family and my country behind, but the memory of God's heart and the rays of light beaming into the darkness of my life brought to my mind a vision of a day when God's Light would pierce through the darkness of Iran, and although darkness will not comprehend it, the Great Light will be able to pull out oceans of souls from the dark pit into His safe and loving embrace.

The people living in darkness have seen a great light; on those living in the land of the shadow of death, a light has dawned.
—Matthew 4:16

This thought warmed my heart and enabled me to sleep in peace.

4

AMERICA—THE OTHER END OF THE EARTH

Come to me, all you who are weary and burdened, and I will give you rest. Take my yoke upon you and learn from me, for I am gentle and humble in heart, and you will find rest for your souls. For my yoke is easy and my burden is light.

—Matthew 11:28-30

We arrived in Amarillo, Texas, in February of 1979. Some of the experiences of my arrival have faded away with time. I don't recall all the specifics. I just remember I felt like a scared little kitten being thrown onto a big stage. The sounds of foreign languages, English and Spanish, cars, and strange people were overwhelming. All the hundreds of people I saw around me were foreigners. I realized I did not know a soul in America!

There were lots of English signs everywhere. In Iran we were lucky if we had signs to tell us what streets we were on. In my few car travels to other cities in Iran, I remembered there were no signs to show the way to exit a town or a way to a specific town. People asked other people, and it was just the word of mouth that was our guide. My early impression of America was how new it looked! I was used to seeing buildings that were two hundred years old! Old brick or stone houses common there. The streets and alleys in Iran were old, muddy, or cobblestone. There were new buildings in Tehran mainly, but I lived in smaller, older cities most of my life, like the ancient Khoozestan (Ilam in the Bible) and Isfahan. I was used to seeing the aged and rundown buildings, four-hundred-year-old bridges, and old mud-straw homes. The newness of America was an astonishing contrast. Everything looked so shiny clean—the buildings, the streets, and even the people!

The streets in Texas were unusually quiet. I do not even remember hearing the sound of a car horn. This was amazing! In Iran, lines on the road were only a mere suggestion. People drove anywhere on the road, outside their lane, and on sidewalks. People in Iran did not cross traffic at crosswalks only—they crossed anywhere, anytime, on the street, in any direction, dodging traffic, lane by lane, while cars honked their horns in protest. You heard car horns day and night. It was normal for us. I never drove in Iran, so when I started learning here, it was no problem. I didn't have to unlearn bad driving habits.

Americans seemed very friendly but unaware of the world I came from. It seemed as if the noise that I was accustomed to didn't exist here. People seemed very detached from the rest of the world. I felt very alone and extremely uncertain and insecure about my future.

I was still in shock. Everything happened so suddenly. I just realized that I was on the other end of the world. I was totally detached from my roots! I suddenly remembered my vow to my God when He presented His heart to me in the night skies of Ahwaz—that, if necessary, I would go to the ends of the earth to find Him. It just sank in! I truly was on the other end of the earth!

I cried a lot when I was at home alone. I was glad we had a small television in our small apartment. I followed the news eagerly. My beloved country had plunged into chaos, and although the shah decided to leave the country and not risk the bloodshed, I still heard news of killings and executions. I was afraid for my father's life. I was also afraid that my brothers would somehow get caught up in the chaos and get killed. Many different political factions had emerged from the underground, and every faction wanted a piece of the pie. Every group wanted control, and so no one trusted anyone. No one knew who was a friend and who was an enemy. The line between a friend and foe was smeared beyond distinction, mostly by the new Islamist conquerors. Many people betrayed their own friends or family just to save their own lives.

My family told me later that they witnessed a side of their countrymen they had never seen. This was heartlessness, ruthlessness, and an absence of basic human integrity and decency. The people's worst was now the norm.

In Farsi, the phrase *harj o marj* means chaos combined with looting, crime, and civil disobedience. That was the state of Iran when I left, and although I was away, my heart ached for the destruction and death I was hearing about in the news. I felt guilty within because I was safe, walking in the peaceful streets of America, when my friends, family, and countrymen in Iran were fighting to stay alive.

After a few months, the victorious Islamic movement unleashed one of the bloodiest campaigns against all those different factions that were against the shah and those who opposed the Islamic state. *Allah's* wrath personified by *Ayatollah Khomeini* and plunged the country to the pit of the seventh-century Arabia. Persia as we knew it had disappeared into history and was replaced by the spirit of darkness.

There was no international phone communication into Iran for a long time. This was first because of the revolution and later because of the Iran-Iraq War. Every time the leaders of a country need to protect themselves and their power, they interrupt all the communications to and from the country. A month or so after arriving in Amarillo, I was able to get a connection for just a minute, long enough to tell my family I was fine and living in the United States safely.

I had lost my family and my country. I had dropped out of my college in Isfahan because of my marriage, and I missed my studies. I no longer had my hobby—reading. Books were now in English, and I did not know the language well enough to read or understand. I missed my father the most. He was the source of strength and security for me.

Amarillo was a nice, quiet city. We had a small two-room rental apartment. I was accustomed to big and spacious housing with all the comfort and conveniences, such as air conditioning. Here, I thought, is my American home—small, simple, and very empty. I had no friends to invite in for lunch and nobody to visit. The only soul I knew was my husband, and he was insensitive to my situation. My marriage was not going well. We were as different as day and night. During the days, I was alone. The phone never rang, and the doorbell remained silent. I spent most of my time daydreaming.

The city was filled with churches—almost one in every block. In Iran, seeing a church was rare, maybe one in a remote area of a big city. I never came across one even though I remember I had a few classmates in high school who were Armenian Christians. They never talked about their faith or their church or invited me to their homes. I had no curiosity about what the church looked like inside or what went on within those walls. Here in America, I saw churches everywhere! I saw the crosses on the rooftops. As an artist, I liked how the cross on the roof completed a building and provided symmetry and thus aesthetic value. It seems like a million years ago when no emotion within my heart was invoked at the sight of a cross. It seems like a million years ago when the sight of a cross on top of a church was totally irrelevant to my life! What it did not do then was what it does now—causes my knees to tremble in awe and adoration!

My extreme loneliness and unhappy marriage caused me to plead for a son—a son who would be mine only and whose love nobody could take away from me. I had my wish; my son was born a few days before Christmas in 1979. It was my first Christmas in America, and I didn't know anything about it. Although I had heard that it was the birthday celebration of the Prophet Jesus, I had no notion of its importance. The Christmas trees, decorated artistically with colorful ornaments, sat in the halls of the hospital and seemed to be waiting for something or someone. I had no knowledge of the meaning or the activities associated with the beautiful trees. I did not see where the birth of Jesus fit into the occasion. Although this finding puzzled me, I blamed it on my unfamiliarity with the American culture.

The first day I held my son in my arms in the hospital, I sang the song I had heard and liked: "You are so beautiful to me." My hospital room was empty—no visitors, flowers, or sounds of laughter. I could not help remembering my sister when she had her first child in Abadan, Iran. My parents bought the biggest flower basket found in Ahwaz and drove to Abadan to be with her for a couple of days. Her room could not hold all the visitors she received, and the child, my beautiful niece, was showered with gold and silver jewelry and the finest baby clothes. The celebration went on for weeks. But somehow, my God comforted me in that empty hospital room, and the gentle face of my son warmed my heart.

The hospital staff tucked my son in a Christmas stocking when we left the hospital. He was such a big boy; he went into the stocking only halfway! I still hang that stocking on the door to his room in my house during Christmas even though he lives far away in Europe with his wife. He was Jesus' gift to me, although, at the time I did not know the Giver! Thankfully, He was patient, faithful, and longsuffering; He waited for me and did not let me go!

Once when my son was only two weeks old, I laid him on the bed to feed him. I had given him a small teddy bear that was a part of the baby crib's carousel. As usual, he was playing with it with his mouth. All of the sudden he was choking. Apparently the teddy bear's eye came off and dropped in his mouth. His face turned purple! My husband put his hands in his small throat and was able to remove it. I was scared to death. I came so close to losing him! I thanked God for saving his life and for giving him back to me.

A year and half later, my daughter was born in the same hospital. The room was still devoid of visitors, gifts, and laughter. But she was my Mother's day gift, and I felt blessed beyond my comprehension of the word blessed.

The early 1980s are remembered for their high unemployment and inflation. The inflation was about 13 percent, and the unemployment rate had reached double digits, 10 percent. People were suffering. I never blamed it on the President Reagan because he was my favorite president. Surprisingly, he still remains my favorite president.

My husband was jobless too, and we drove south to Houston and then to San Antonio in search of employment. Texas was as big as Iran! Going from one end to the other end took a whole day or more. I liked the fact that there were areas along the roads called rest area. Some had restrooms and washrooms, and some had only a few picnic tables. I thought it was so interesting that someone had thought of tired travelers.

Once in our way to Austin, we stopped at a rest area. The area was just a table and two stony benches above a rocky hill. The children were only two and three years old. They loved to climb the rocks and play with the sand. The day was very hot, and I was tired and weary. We had been on the road for a couple of months now searching for jobs and were running out of money. I was worried about the children and our future. I sat down on a rock to rest while the kids played. I looked next to me, where I sat and noticed a very small red booklet about two inches long. Curiously, I picked it up and looked at the cover. It read, "Bible Verses—Comfort, Assurance, Salvation." I opened it and it read,

> *Come unto me all ye that labor and are heavy laden, and I will give you rest.*
> —Matthew 11:28

> *Casting all your care upon him; for he cares for you.*
> —1 Peter 5:7

This little booklet became my treasured possession. It reaffirmed that my God who gave me His heart long ago still knew where I was and still cared for me. He knows that I am tired and weary of this life. I knew He was watching over me in this foreign country. Although I was not a Christian, I knew finding that little Bible booklet, as I called it, in the middle of nowhere was good news. I believe this was the prelude of my finding the ultimate good news! It was God's way of comforting me. I still have this booklet today. It reminds me of a time when I was still traveling through life in the dark, seeking the light, and the Spirit of God was going before me to keep me on schedule and to make preparation for the final appointment, where I would receive the final deliverance!

We did not find employment in Austin, so we headed to San Antonio. My husband found a job, and we settled down.

A rest for the weary traveler at a Texas rest area.

I liked San Antonio. It was a friendly town and full of possibilities.

Once the children turned four and five years old, I enrolled them in a preschool and kindergarten, and I started school again myself. My two years of college in Iran were not accepted since I had no transcripts with me. They insisted on seeing proof of grades. I told them about the Revolution and later the war between Iran and Iraq and why it was impossible to get transcripts, but they did not accept my reasons, so I started from scratch.

Ironically, my new college was called, "The Incarnate Word." Of course, I didn't have a clue what it meant. It was a Catholic school, and I had a few nuns and priests as my professors. Not one ever mentioned Jesus and His mission. I was not overly curious about the name of my college since my English was very limited. I just figured this is just another unfamiliar English word. I was in the dark still, and as the Word says, "The darkness has not understood it" (John 1:5).

I did not know anything about the Catholic Church or other denominations. I saw them all as Christians. Mostly I thought the Catholics were the strict practitioners of the Christianity, as I had seen in American movies in Iran. I enrolled my children in a Catholic school because I desired for them to grow in a good environment. After the first year, the school administrator, a nun, asked me if the children were baptized.

"No," I said. "We are not Christians!"

She looked very perplexed! "What about your husband?" she said.

"He is a Jew, and I am a Muslim," I said.

She looked even more perplexed and said, "This school is for Catholics only." So we enrolled the children in the public school.

Since I was a self-taught artist in Iran, I took advantage of the art classes at my college. One of those classes was the ceramic class. It turned out that I was a natural potter! What took other students days to make on the potter's wheel took me only minutes. My teacher was very pleased. One of the students thought my talent was in my Persian blood since it is the ancient land of pottery.

Once at the completion of a term, I made a beautiful cross for my favorite algebra teacher, Sister Grubber. I made it out of porcelain clay—the finest clay—shaped it, carved it, and then glazed it with a very elegant mother-of-pearl glaze. I then hand painted it with a tiny brush using an expensive gold glaze over the carvings and the edges. It was a beautiful artwork for me, and I knew she would love it, but I had no clue about its meaning or significance.

I was studying in a Catholic school, populated with nuns and priests. I took two years of Bible studies and interacted with people who obviously had heard of Jesus all their lives. During that time, I never heard the story of the cross! After two years, I transferred to St. Mary's University. Again, it was a Catholic school and I had professors who were priests and nuns, and again, no one shared with me the story of the cross and the love that came down.

I finished my studies in December of '89, right when my father came to America for his cancer treatment.

My Father's Visit

In December 1989, the job market was not good. Besides, my cancer-stricken father came to Texas to see his grandchildren and to see me for the first time in ten years, and I was not looking to start a career at this particular time.

I was, however, working part time for a local real estate lawyer. Howard was a very compassionate and loving lawyer. He helped everyone regardless of one's ability to pay. He used to even accept nonmonetary payment such as books, farm products, etc., from the poor and the widows who couldn't afford the price of legal services. He was especially sympathetic toward the women who were mistreated by their husbands. He was the one everyone could count on in times of trouble and need. With his busy law practice, he managed to also be a volunteer Emergency Responder for years. Howard was witty and generous too. Once when I had just joined his team, we went for lunch to a nearby café. When I pulled open my purse to pay for my meal, he stopped me and with a smile and said, "I don't pay you enough! I'll get it!" And so he often paid my way or even for my children when we joined him for social events.

When Howard heard about my father's cancer, the facts about his condition in Iran, and my financial situation, he wrote a letter to a US senator from Texas to seek help with granting him visa for medical purposes. Then he co-signed a loan for me so I could buy tickets to go to Turkey to bring him to the United States for medical treatment.

I arrived in Istanbul, Turkey, on a cold, windy day. I was picked me up from the airport and taken to the motel where my father was. I knew I was going to see my father after more than ten years, but I could not be happy because I knew he was suffering from cancer and the shadow of death was crawling near. One cannot experience joy in the presence of sadness. My sadness was the state of my father's health. He was dying.

I arrived to the motel room where my father was lying in bed. I did not recognize him. I looked at the other side of the room, and there was nobody else. This old and sick man was my father. I sat down by his bed, trying to hold the tears from falling. He was helped to a higher position, and when he saw me, he started crying like a child, but he was too weak even to cry; he didn't have the strength at all. He came closer to kiss my face, but his lips just touched my face and he didn't have strength to actually kiss. That was when I lost control of my tears.

I still could not resolve the conflict I had in my mind. On one side of my brain, I was seeing my father of ten years ago who was strong, tall, and handsome, with his famous smile, and on the other side of my brain I was seeing this small, fragile, sick, and old man! I could not reconcile the two pictures in my mind.

My father started to explain to me the history of his cancer. With much difficulty, he started to draw on a piece of paper where the tumor was, and he wrote some words. After only a few seconds of writing, I cried when I saw his *lam*—that is "L" in one of the words. My father's handwriting was unique, and especially, his *lams* were one of a kind. That moment was when it clicked that this man was my father! I just connected with the one I left behind when I saw him write the way I remembered. He had lost over 70 percent of his weight, and the tall, stout, and formidable man I knew had turned into a small, fragile, hundred-pound skeleton! The cancer was eating him away.

We flew to the United States after a few days. God gave him extraordinary strength for the trip. He was surprised himself by the new energy he found within himself to walk and endure the hours of flight. He perfectly lived up to his name—a mountain-born!

At the San Antonio's airport, my husband came to pick us up. He found me at the baggage area and asked me where my father was. I pointed to the end of the hall where all the chairs were and a few people as well as my father were sitting. He looked from right to left and then to the right again, but he didn't recognize anyone as my father. I pointed to the one sitting with a cane in his hand. He shook his head from disbelief.

We went home, and my father met my children for the first time.

Off to the Next Waypoint

I received a couple of letters from the US Navy that indicated an interest in interviewing me, but I discarded every one of them because I was not ready to think of a job away from Texas since I was taking care of my father. Months passed, and I did not return any requests for calls or information.

One day during work at Howard's law office, I got a call from Virginia. I spoke to a lady who wanted to talk to me about a permanent job with the US government. Apparently she had called home and my father had answered the phone, and with broken English, he was able to understand the call and give my phone number at the office.

My father insisted that I should go for the interview even though I would be away for at least forty-eight hours. I was reluctant to go, since he was very sick and he needed help for the smallest tasks. The children were only eight and nine years old. My husband was there, but since we had problems, I wasn't counting on his help. But my father insisted. He knew that this was an opportunity of a lifetime.

So I did. I went to the interview, and they offered me a position as a scientist on spot! When I came home and told my father, he was excited. I had not seen his excitement since decades ago back in Khoozestan. Though he was weak and weary, I recognized the twinkling light in his eyes when he was happy for his child. He knew that I needed to take care of my children and myself. He could tell that my marriage wasn't going well. He was glad that I was able to make a living all on my own. His whole life he worked to ensure his children's future and prosperity.

Years later, I heard that when Iran was in its early revolutionary experience and also at war with Iraq, everyone was worried about me being here alone and unprotected. My brother-in-law asked my father why was it that he did not seem to worry as much as others. He answered them, "Because she used to read a lot of books. She knows about people!"

My father left the United States after only two months. His last wish, seeing his grandchildren and myself for the last time, was granted. He wanted to die in his own country in the midst of his larger family. He left with tears in his eyes, and I knew I would not see him ever again. I had enough time to get a picture of his plane at the airport. In those days, we were free to go with the passengers all the way to the gate.

A few months after, weary and exhausted from life's many trials—the loss of my country, my family, the terminal cancer of my father and his condition, my dysfunctional marriage and upcoming divorce, the two small children who didn't understand any of this, and my mountain of financial debt—I packed my household and set to travel across the country to Virginia.

My good friend Gail was worried about me and opposed to my move to such a faraway state. She was worried about the children, but I told her that God knew me personally, and knew my situation, and would take care of me. I told her the Creator of the universe had shown His love to me, and again and again walked with me, even to a remote insignificant rest area near Austin, and had saved my son's life twice. He will see me through. We packed our bags in our old '79 yellow Chevy Impala station wagon and left for Virginia.

5

When It Rains, It Pours!

In the time of my favor I heard you, and in the day of salvation I helped you. I tell you, now is the time of God's favor, now is the day of Salvation
—*2 Corinthians 6:2*

Grace. God's grace. It's a seemingly simple word, yet it is incomprehensible by the human mind. It is unearnable by any human merit, no matter how noble, and incomparable to any reward received for any reason anywhere on earth.

In my thirty-plus years of living in the United States, I have heard, read, and known this word to a level where I believed I grasped its meaning. It was always a nice and elegant word. But that was all—a nice and elegant word, just like many other nice and elegant words in the English language. There was a moment in history, a defining moment in my life, twenty years ago in 1990 when my eyes were opened. The chains of bondage broke loose, the veil over my heavily burdened heart rolled away, and I stepped into the light—the light of the Son!

For the first time in my life, my heart was filled with the joy of my God—a joy unspeakable. My mind opened into a new freedom of thinking beyond the limitations of logic; my soul began singing from the depth of my being with thousands of instruments—a harmonious symphony. The singing within never stopped! It continues. My lips joined the symphony, continuously praising His holy name. My hands are lifted toward heaven in praise and exaltation; my knees are bent, unable to stand straight; and my head is bowed in reverence and worship. Body, mind, and soul, I was immersed in God's grace and transformed into a new being with a posture of belief and adoration. Joyful tears of salvation poured down my cheeks like a long-sought rain over a dry land. I never knew how thirsty I was till I was completely soaked in the pouring rain of His grace.

The dryness of any land is compared to a wetland. If there is no land other than an arid desert, that is, no other state of being, then the dry land does not know of its dryness. If one has always lived in a cave where there is no light, then one does not know or miss the light since it is not a part of one's reality. So is the state of a person who is empty within; it feels normal since the emptiness is the only reality known, and nothing other than emptiness is ever experienced. Once I was filled with my Savior's grace, for the first time I knew I was *found* by God, although, I never knew I was *lost* until that moment! I realized I was in the darkness all along only after I stepped into the infinitely brilliant light of the Son.

The day of my salvation was in November 1990. I was at work in my small cubicle at a small naval laboratory in northern Virginia. That was my first year working for the navy as a computer scientist. I loved my new work and my new home. My home was in a paradise of my own. This was the start of a new chapter in my life!

Sam, a colleague at the time, and now a longtime friend, shared the good news of Jesus Christ with me. It did not make complete sense to me, though. In Islam, we were taught that Jesus was a prophet just like Abraham, Moses, and Mohammed. We believed that Jesus was a good man, a good teacher, and the son of Mary. We learned the Holy Bible was written by mere men, changed several times over centuries, and thus could not be the Word of God. Its credibility ranked lower than the Qur'an, which, we were taught, was given to Mohammed through God's angel. Saying that Jesus died for my sins or for anyone's sins, or that He was the Son of God, did not make much sense to me, especially since the Qur'an says, "God has no child and is not a child of anyone" (Q 112:1-4). It was taught that the Qur'an was the ultimate revelation of God and Islam was the ultimate religion—the completion and the perfection of all religions.

Sam had no clue about the heavy baggage I was carrying or my struggle to make sense out of Christianity and Islam. He had no knowledge of Islam's doctrine and its theology and the heavy fear and burden that was a part of every Muslim's daily life. Sam did not see the apparent nonsense of the gospel that I saw at the time. The crucifixion was a form of execution used in ancient times, so what was the big deal about a prophet getting executed? Most prophets, followers of prophets, or just men who would go against the establishment usually get killed. What I did not know was first, who Jesus really was, and second, that the crucifixion was not about just the physical torture or murder; it was about sin—mankind's sin. It was as though I was trying to write a totally new story on top of a heavily soiled and old, scribbled piece of paper!

> *No one tears a patch from a new garment and sews it on an old one. If he does, he will have torn the new garment, and the patch from the new will not match the old. And no one pours new wine into old wineskins. If he does, the new wine will burst the skins, the wine will run out and the wineskins will be ruined. No, new wine must be poured into a new wineskins.*
> —Luke 5:36-38

At the time, I was trying to fit what Sam was telling me about Jesus Christ into my old belief system based on what I was taught about Islam, and even Christianity, in Iran. I was limiting my appreciation for this new information and diluting it with my old religious beliefs and notions. I slowly realized that Jesus offers something new—something requiring a fresh sprit. It was a new story requiring a new piece of a paper. I could not simply write it on an already-scribbled old piece of paper!

For the first time, through several conversations with Sam, I heard it was not just my deeds on earth that made me sinful. Rather, sin was in my blood; therefore, I could not escape it, no matter how much I would try. Then I heard the story of Jesus, who bore the sins of mankind while on the cross. And if that was not shocking enough, Jesus, I heard, was the Son of God who came to earth as a man!

Although these revelations were too much, too abstract, and too supernatural for me to instantly comprehend and believe, there was something special about that moment in my life. I believe it was then that the seed of the truth was planted in my mind and spirit, though I was not fully aware of the extent of it.

Muslims believe that the miracles that Jesus performed, were done by God using Jesus, just as they believe the miracles that Moses performed, were done by God through Moses. Muslims also believe that Christianity is a religion of Westerners or foreigners and that Muslims cannot be Christian (or even think about it) because Muslims are Muslims. They believe there is a type or a compatibility issue. It was like a camel wanting to become a horse or an orange wanting to become an apple. Impossible! The idea of conversion, I remember, was never an option. They instilled in us that we are Muslims by birth, by nature, by race, and by nationality. The non-Muslim Iranians were either Armenians who fled to Iran decades before from the north or Jews who were descendants of pre-Islamic exiles who settled there and never went back to the Promised Land. In other words, these non-Muslim Iranians had an excuse, a reason why they were not Muslims living in Iran; it was not their fault that they were not Muslims.

I had another work colleague, Tim, who is now a close friend of mine; he was a missionary in the Ukraine for several years. One day in the same year, during a few minutes of office talk about the fall of the USSR, I said, "No matter what, we are doomed!"

Tim, with a sweet and a confident smile, said, "I know I will be OK!" His confidence struck me and stuck in my mind.

In Islam, even though we were taught it was the best, the most complete, and the greatest religion of all, we never could say with confidence we would be OK after death. No one knew the way to be OK! At Iranian funerals, the mourners would say, "*khoda biamorzesh,*" which means, "May God save him." Although good deeds, paying the *zakat,* or tithe, and going to Mecca could all help, the road to salvation was not defined. The interesting thing was that not having a defined way to salvation was not a problem for me, since we were not told that Christianity or any other religion had a defined way. The unknowable God in Islam, who is also the merciful, would be just if He wishes. The problem was that this unknowable God was also an angry and ready-to-punish God; we never knew what to expect, because Allah was unpredictable since he was unknowable.

Also, this lack of a way to salvation was not a big problem for me because I was unaware of our sinful nature. If the sin issue, as we believed in Iran, was about sinning as adults, then it explains why we thought that by trying to be as good as possible, we might be OK after death. All one had to do was follow the tenets of Islam, be good and moral (defined by leaders of Islam or yourself), maximize good deeds, and perform religious duties. This would maximize one's likelihood of going to heaven.

Looking back, I can see why Iranian funerals were so the end of everything! The weeping and wailing of women and their purposeful wounding of their faces with their fingernails now clearly portrays their hopelessness. I liked Tim's assurance, but I still did not know why or how he was so sure.

Back to my day of salvation! Later that November, I saw an advertisement in the local newspaper requesting entries for a poetry publication. The subject was any social issue. My intention was to write a poem addressing the troubled life of teenagers in America. Having gone through these critical years in my native country, I had a special compassion for the youth and felt that I knew and understood some of the sources of this trouble.

That day at work during my lunch break, I picked up a pen and a clean sheet of paper and started to write. As I started, I noticed that the subject matter that I was writing about was not what I intended, but I was writing nevertheless. The writing was too smooth, too easy to be true. My thoughts were on the paper before I even thought them! I dare say they were not even my thoughts that were penned on the paper. In a matter of minutes, I was done. I looked at the paper and noticed that I wrote about abortion. I did not write about the issue of abortion; not about the abortion of America's teens; and not even about the ethical dimension of abortion. I wrote about my own abortion from fifteen years ago—the one that I never talked to anyone about, not even to God. It was the event that I taught myself to forget, or so I thought!

My tears were pouring down, smearing the ink on the paper. Long ago, I had packed this event, wrapped it with a cloth of shame and guilt, and pushed it to the farthest corner of my mind, hoping it would eventually fade away from my memory. I had not thought about it for years. I thought I overcame the pain and the shame.

I knew it was God! This was His work. He chose the subject, and He inspired its composition. It was a poem of confession, inspired and written by the finger of God, the Holy Spirit! I witnessed it all. He was reminding me that storing old guilt and hiding it will not do me any good; I had to face it with God. The matter was not closed with Him! How could it be? One of His most helpless children was murdered and another was carrying the guilt years after. The consequence was my separation from Him. He wanted an end to this separation. He wanted to convict me, to hear my admittance of guilt, and most importantly, my repentance. He was ready to forgive me only if I was ready to come clean with Him! I will never forget the poem I wrote that day with the Lord's inspiration:

> Ponds of mourning,
> Rivers of regret
> Seas of untold stories
>
> Washing out the sins of past
> Tears, blended softly in fears,

> Oh, no, the baby's killed,
> Pitiless ripped
> Torn, inside the mother's womb
>
> The dreams of murder
> Breaking the silent dawn
> The dawn of prayers, of tears, of wishes
> The dawn of the passing Son

I noticed a few of amazing things about this poem.

First, God reminded me of the dreams of murder I had following the abortion. It is true. As I mentioned earlier, I was married to my German-American husband who worked in Iran and who had a troubled past. It took me years to get a grip of his sorrowful past. He wanted me to have an abortion for various reasons that amounted to being an inconvenience for him. I was strongly opposed to it, but I agreed to it because I was very young and inexperienced, because I was cut off from my family for marrying a foreigner, and because of various marital problems that were weighing so heavily on me. I had nightmares of murdering my own child for months after the abortion but tried to bury the experience in my mind and did not tell a soul. I carried the pain and guilt but never spoke of it to anyone.

I must add that my opposition to abortion at the time is not the same type of opposition I have now. I was opposed to it because culturally and morally it did not agree with my upbringing. It had nothing to do with God. My eyes could not see, my mind could not think, and my heart could not feel what this meant to God. Although at the time I knew He existed, I did not know Him personally! I did not know His heart. I did not know Him as my Father. I did not know what life meant to Him. I did not know that He wove that life in me. I had no idea that the child I was carrying was wonderfully made and made in His image!

Second, I noticed "the passing Son" was spelled with a capital S. God referred to my son as His Son! It was clear to me that I broke His heart as much as when His heart broke at the passing of His one and only Son on the cross. What an amazing love He has for His most helpless children!

Third, I quickly became aware that God wrote that poem. For years I had rejected the authority of the Holy Bible based on the "it is men-written" premise, yet God threw out that belief from my mind when He caused me to write the words that were not mine yet penned by me. The topic was thousands of years and thousands of miles away from my mind, yet He brought it to the forefront of my being. God, I concluded, could do whatever He wants to do. He can use people to write whatever He wishes them to write. He wrote the Bible using people. What a freedom to know and to live with this truth!

Later, after my new birth in Christ, I read, "All scripture is God-breathed and is useful for teaching, rebuking, correcting and training in righteousness" (2 Tim 3:16).

Most Iranians of the pre-revolution period can easily remember the excitement of getting up in the early morning and traveling miles to a friend's or family's house who owned a television just to see the boxing match of the World Heavyweight Champion, Mohammad Ali. The room would be packed with young fans, and mothers would prepare food to keep the party alive. As the crowd watched, Mohammed Ali would throw a few of his strong blows against the opponent. With each blow, the opponent would become weaker and more convinced of the champion's power. Then it would come—the final blow. The opponent would fall to the ground, with no strength to stand. The final punch would be too powerful and very effective! At that moment, the match would be over. There would be no ambiguities of who the most powerful boxer was—no doubt who the champion was.

And so it was for me; I experienced God's evidence for His existence, for His love, and for His sovereignty in my life. Yet this experience with the poem was the final and most powerful "punch" that threw me to the ground and caused me to bow down and to open my eyes to the truth of Jesus Christ.

My knees fell to the ground, with my head down and with tears pouring down my face. I recalled what Sam said about Jesus who forgives. I knew He was calling me, and He definitely got my attention! The light of the world shined on me with its most intense and purest light!

At that moment, I was absolutely certain that Jesus Christ is God, that Jesus Christ is my Lord and Savior! For the first time, I asked for God's forgiveness, and He pointed me to the cross where my sins were nailed! The cross was no longer just a method of execution; it was not just a symbol of a religion or an icon for architectural symmetry. It was where God bore my sins, where His holy and precious blood poured out for me. It all finally made sense to me! Somehow the story of the cross became a part of my new blood.

Grace poured on me like a massive rainstorm! I was filled with God's love like a balloon filled with air about to burst. I sought the truth—the ultimate truth of my life. Now here, in this new continent, on the other end of the world, I came face to face with it. Truth, I discovered, is a person—and His name is Jesus! I had no idea that He had said it Himself, long ago.

> *"I am the way, the truth, and the life. No one comes to the Father but through me."*
> —*John 4:16*

I came to believe without a shadow of a doubt that Jesus Christ was the Savior of the world and of me, personally. God's grace came full circle. I finally found the one who gave me His heart over twenty years ago in Ahwaz! It was my turn now. Happily and tearfully, I gave Him my heart! My imperfect and broken heart; my tired, bruised, and lonely heart! I gave it to the only true God who patiently waited for me. The young Persian girl who used to look up to the heavens from her lowly balcony in Iran in search of her Creator just reached the end of her quest in America. I was finally home!

At the time of this day of salvation, I had not read the Bible, had not heard a preacher, and did not know anything about the Trinity, but the knowledge of God was written on my heart as I walked on the path to salvation. I knew with all certainty that the Creator who gave me His heart twenty years ago, the Son who saved my soul, and the Spirit who guided my writing of the poem were all one and the same—one true triune God.

Clothed in Christ's righteousness, I now stand before my heavenly Father forgiven, redeemed, and free!

And where the Lord is, there is freedom.
—*2 Corinthians 3:17*

The lost sheep is finally reunited with her Good Shepherd! The Savior's words are ringing in my ear like a heavenly hymn:

"You will know the truth, and the truth shall set you free!"
—*John 8:32*

My heart sings continuous songs of worship, redemption, and forgiveness all wrapped in a beautiful choir of love. The hymnist sings the song of my soul:

> When peace like a river attended my way,
> When sorrows like sea billows roll,
> Whatever my lot, Thou hast taught me to say,
> It is well; it is well, with my soul
>
> My sin, O, the bliss of this glorious thought
> My sin, not in part, but the whole,
> Is nailed to the cross, and I bear it no more,
> Praise the Lord, praise the Lord, O my soul!

Recently, I wrote this poem praising the Lord for my church's Bible study:

> Oh Jesus, my soul sings for joy
> For You have freed me
> For You have delivered me
> For You have made me Your own
>
> Oh Jesus, my eyes long for You
> For You saw me in the dark
> For You showed me Your heart
> For You handed me Your love
>
> Oh Jesus, my lips praise You
> For You have saved me from the pit
> For You have lifted me from despair
> For You have washed me from my sin

Oh Jesus, my hands are lifted up to You
For You have brought me joy
For You have brought me peace
For You have brought me life

Oh Savior, my knees are bowed to You
For You came down for me
For You were nailed to the Cross
For You shed Your blood for me

Oh Jesus, my life is all for You
For it was bought by You
For it is blessed by You
For it is lived for You

I welcomed the ultimate peace to my soul! Nothing compares with this peace. It is like a heavenly river that sprinkles fresh, clean water on my face. Its essence has the sweet fragrance of the Lily of the Valley, and it tastes like honey. It is everlasting peace from the very source—the Prince of Peace!

6

Betrayed... Big Time!

Do not believe every spirit, but test the spirits to see whether they are from God, because many false prophets have gone out into the world.
—1 John 4:1

As I walked ahead in the Light of the Son, I looked back to where I had been.

The darkness was incredibly thick! It resembled the thickness of the heavy burdens of my heart before the Son lifted them and nailed them to His cross. I remembered how the darkness had caused my eyes to be blinded to my surroundings, blinded to the truth, and separated from my Lord. The same darkness had caused too many hearts to be filled with guilt, bitterness, and hatred. It had caused so many healthy minds to be captive to false teachers and false doctrines, to be chained and enslaved to the forces of evil. The popular American saying, "A mind is a terrible thing to waste," applied perfectly to what I had recognized happening to millions of great Iranian minds.

The darkness was so deep and heavy that the people's worship of their creator was reduced to the kissing the cover of a dusty old Qur'an and observing a few fasting days that included in parroting a few verses in Arabic, a foreign language to most Muslims.

I was aware of the fact that darkness covered numerous crimes against humanity, especially against women. In times of religious anniversary of *Moharram*, men chained and often slashed themselves as a form of suffering for Imam Hussein, the dead imam who was murdered by his enemies for the cause of Islam in AD 680. The faithful called his so-called martyrdom a sacrifice, but no one can dispute the fact that he did not go to his death for any other human being. He was killed in the Battle of Karbala (a city in Iraq) by his opponents for power on earth and for pleasing Allah. Pleasing Allah by martyrdom was, according to Islam, his guarantee to paradise! Yet men beat themselves, sometimes to the point of exhaustion, and suffer dehydration or even death just to show and prove their faithfulness.

The way the evil had twisted their mindset was incredible! In their homes, these men, were abusers, tyrants, and selfish husbands and fathers.

The hypocrisy and senselessness of their show and tell of their religious rituals should have raised a red flag in my mind, but if there was one, it couldn't be seen in the darkness of my world.

As the cold tears of regret poured down my face and blurred my vision, I looked deeper into the darkness behind me. At its heart ruled a formidable force who was neither slow with anger nor abounding with love! In fact, this force was so quick in anger and abounding in hate, distrust, and unfaithfulness that any insult or disrespect to him was considered apostasy and thus punishable by death!

The hearts of its followers were filled with hatred and envy for Christians and Jews. The core of the darkness was made of solid deception. It was a systematic, purposeful, and well-designed deception that savagely raped millions of my countrymen of their souls, of their eternal future. People were lied to and deceived to think that there is nothing good beyond the frames of Islam—no hope, no Messiah, no atonement for sin, no resurrection, and no salvation.

We were, as Islam taught, at the mercy of the so-called merciful Allah. This same merciful Allah hates all non-Muslims to a point that only their shed blood satisfies him (Q 9:5), and according to Qur'an, he also told Mohammed that women are made for "play" for men: "your wives are as a tilth [a piece of land to be plowed] unto you, so approach your tilth when and how you will" (Q 2:223).

In the Qur'an, as well as in Hadith (next to Qur'an, the most sacred book-collection of sayings of Mohammed), Mohammad states, "Wives are play things, so take your pick," and "At the mercy of Allah who entitled women to only half of legal rights of men" (Q 2:228, 4:11, 2:282 and Hadith3.826). We were at the mercy of Allah who, according to Qur'an, sends all people, good or bad, righteous or criminal, to hell first (Q 19:71), and then determines whom he wills to be in paradise with him.

As I cried over the life lost in the vast emptiness of my darkened universe, where neither hope nor love had a true existence, I realized that the great thief of ages is trembling over my repetitious utterance of the name of Jesus, who freed me from the enslavement and who rescued me from the grip of the old serpent who was determined to pull me to his deep pit and separate me forever from my Lord.

> *For He has rescued us from the dominion of darkness and brought us into the kingdom of the Son he loves...*
> —*Colossians 1:13*

I believe the most urgent and terrorizing moment for Satan is when he is faced with one of his prisoners "defecting" to God's side! He uses all the schemes and tricks available to him to overshadow the new joy in the heart of the new believer.

As for me, he gave me an aftertaste that was bitter and sickening.

I realized that I had been betrayed big time. I realized that I was deceived and lied to all my life. This deception was designed cleverly by Satan, implemented forcefully and violently by Mohammed, and executed systematically by Islamic leaders until today. It has caused over a billion people to rely on their own self-righteousness to obtain access to heaven and has reduced the one and only Savior of the world to a mere prophet, even lesser than the illiterate, opportunist, war-monger, so-called prophet of Islam!

This realization first brought me anger and despair and then disappointment and great sorrow in the first months of my new birth.

The memory of waking up at the edge of dawn with a rhythmic, musical call of prayer and inhaling the crisp air of early morning all to demonstrate my devotion to God played in my mind like an old movie. My mother and I and other family members enjoyed the early-morning feast called *sahari*. She would spend hours of labor preparing the delicious Persian rice and side dishes just so we all would eat and nourish our bodies for the fasting period. My father's pride to see his young daughters so committed to observe the religious duties was the high reward. We finished the morning feast with the usual prayer ritual to start the fasting. I remembered how I looked forward to the evening's *Iftar*—the break of fasting. There was a mystic feeling of warmth to the event, as I recall, that I personally contributed to the heavenly realm of the fasting. I remembered the innocence of my desires to please my God whose name, I believed, was Allah. The prayers were performed facing Mecca. Prayer verses in Arabic were memorized, and I repeated them like a parrot, thinking they were directed to the Creator of universe.

Now, for the first time with my seeing eyes, I saw clearly all the features of a perfect design to deceive, manipulate, and lie. It was the ultimate betrayal! I saw how cleverly it was implemented into the hearts and minds of people.

And so, I embarked on a challenging task of identifying the key elements of this deception and the strategy that was used to control the minds and hearts of my Muslim countrymen and others around the world.

I set to identify all of the Islam's falsehoods—its god, its prophet, and its doctrine. I was also motivated to identify the trademarks of a deliberate deception. I knew I could do this. I wasn't blind anymore, and besides, I had the Spirit of God within me as my Helper.

Truth Distorted

We all know how Satan works. We know his schemes, his lies, and his strategies. Satan takes God's truth, manipulates it, and changes it to deceive people and to turn them away from the true God. Satan, unlike the true God, doesn't care whether people are in his dark kingdom out of pure ignorance, deception, or lies. Satan doesn't care what one believes or doesn't believe as long as it is not a belief in the true God. In fact, anyone who is not in the kingdom of God is, by definition, in the kingdom of Satan.

Satan's most typical strategy is to smear the truth, manipulate it, twist it, and change it in a way that a person would believe as truth (because it may have some of the elements of the truth), but in reality the person is misguided since he is now operating on the basis of falsehood. Satan mimics God's work or word but distorts it (if he didn't distort it, it would be the truth and by definition, non-satanic) to achieve his own goal, and that is to steal souls.

People live in his dark kingdom, most of them not even knowing it, and that is even more desirable for him. Remember, it is not necessary for Satan to have anyone who by choice rejects God or by choice accepts Satan. All it takes to be a part of his dark kingdom is to believe in anything other than the truth of God.

So knowing the truth of God is the key. It is not a surprise that Satan's effort is to keep people from reading, hearing, and knowing the truth! That is why it is against the law in some Islamic nations to profess, witness, and share Jesus Christ with people! That is why Christians or Christianity are so controlled, suppressed, and unwelcomed. That is why Muslims who decide to follow Christ are jailed and killed by their own leaders and governments or even families.

Part of becoming a US citizen is learning American history. I learned that America was founded under Christian beliefs. However, in today's world of political correctness, invoking the name of God, Jesus, or His Word in some public or government forums in America can be a problem or even viewed as offensive, intolerant, and discriminatory. However, if the same people, in the same forums, mention anything about any other non-Christian religion, that would be viewed as healthy diversity and virtuous open-mindedness. I would argue this is the case because Satan's aim is to keep people from the true God.

Satan uses anything at his disposal to deprive people of the joy of knowing the true God, from a small, seemingly harmless planting of a doubt as he did with Eve in the Garden of Eden to driving the establishment of a religion that results in over a billion of lost souls simply by using one man's political and militaristic ambitions in a land of pagans!

If only I, as a Muslim, had known that God had warned us about this in His Word:

> *Watch out for false prophets. They come to you in sheep's clothing, but inwardly they are ferocious wolves. By their fruit you will recognize them. Do people pick grapes from thorn bushes, or figs from thistles? Likewise, every good tree bears good fruit; but a bad tree bears bad fruit. A good tree cannot bear bad fruit, nor can a bad tree bear good fruit (Matt 7:15-19).*

Again, that is precisely why Islamic leaders keep their people away from Christians, do not permit Christians to speak of Jesus to Muslims, permit and promote the burning of churches, and arrest and kill any Muslim who accepts Christianity. Satan is not only behind the falsehood of Islam, but he is also working 24/7 to keep it from being exposed. His method includes keeping people thinking they are working toward the goal of paradise without offering a clear way, keeping people interested in religion and its do's and don'ts, and his ultimate goal, keeping people from knowing the truth expressed in the person of Jesus Christ.

The Falsehood of Islam

According to Western and non-Western sources, Islam is one of the three monotheistic religions, next to Christianity and Judaism. This means these three religions believe that there is only one God. It also *implies* that the three religions worship the same God, just through different prophets and different tenets or practices. Muslims especially enjoy this assertion because it makes Islam equal (in quality and truthfulness) to

Christianity and Judaism (from an external perspective), and from and internal perspective (within the Islamic world), they believe it surpasses that of Judaism and Christianity because Allah's revelation is finally completed and made perfect in Islam, and Mohammed is the "seal of prophets."

The majority of the secular world is at loss as to why there is so much tension in the world if the three religions worship the same God.

Well, the basis of this question (the three religions worship the same God) is incorrect, and so the question is invalid.

This gross misconception, however, has provided a fertile soil to plow the minds and the hearts of the people and plant the seed of deception and has allowed it to grow, make roots, and bear fruits—fruits of hatred, resentment and distrust toward others, sadness, emptiness, and loneliness.

Once I was out of the shadow of Islam and under the protective umbrella of grace, I started to reflect back to see why and how I was deceived. I always thought of myself as intelligent and reasonable person, and I was angry and yet curious to how I was deceived so effectively, so transparently for many years. With direct access to the throne of God, I prayed for clear and focused mind and open eyes and ears, and I studied the Qur'an and Hadith thoroughly.

For the first time, with my seeing eyes, I saw exactly how over a billion people were and still are deceived purposefully, intentionally, and systematically. I first saw how Satan managed to falsely portray to the people of the world that Allah is just another word for God, the one who made heaven and earth, the one who created Adam and Eve, and the one who spoke to Abraham. I further found out why this is absolutely false. I realized this falsehood by discovering how different the nature of Allah is from the nature of YHWH. The Qur'an, Allah's word, shows this difference clearly.

Included in this campaign against God was the clear picture of how Satan portrayed Mohammed as a prophet of God to implement his own deceptive work. There is a lot of evidence to show that he was a false prophet who was advancing Satan's work instead of God's. He was a useful tool for Satan to distort the ultimate truth.

The false doctrine is another element of this deception. The false doctrine written in Qur'an has imprisoned and blinded Muslims for centuries. This falsehood has led to the many strongholds chained around the throats of innocent Muslims, and many have been suffocated to death as a result.

In the following paragraphs, the result of my research into the falsehood of Islam is presented. I have embedded evidence for purposeful deception in each "falsehood" section where appropriate.

As I stated in the introductory chapter, this book is not intended to be an apologetic in its nature and purpose. However, to describe my spiritual journey and the emotional turbulence associated with the discovery of Islam's falsehood, I must present some apologetic discussion. This discussion serves as the backbone of my belief that Islam is a product of a well-designed, well-engineered deception plot by Satan to keep people from knowing their Savior and knowing the only way to salvation.

I. Allah—a False God

As mentioned earlier, many Westerners and non-Westerners, Muslims or non-Muslims, have come to believe that when one worships Allah, one worships God, since Allah is a generic Arabic word for God. This presupposition of a false common ground generates a false sense of security for people to believe that no matter what our differences are, all roads lead to the same God and there is no need to be alarmed.

In light of America's current politically correct environment, this assertion provides for an easier, less confrontational discussion, and in general, it makes people feel good. It softens the oppositional tone, it smoothes the rough edges of distinctions between different belief systems, and it calms the hostile post-9/11 debates.

But is this the truth, and does the truth matter?

The answers to these two questions are a strong no and yes respectively.

I discovered that the God of the Holy Bible, who is the God of Abraham, Isaac, and Jacob, the God of Moses, and the Father of Jesus, is *not* the same person as the Allah of the Qur'an, the god of Mohammad! This was a shocking truth!

How did I find this out?

Simple. I figured if the nature and character of Allah, according to his own word, the Qur'an, matches perfectly with the nature and character of YHWH according to His own Word, the Bible, then these names point to the same person.

Let's simplify the understanding of this with a few of examples.

Example 1: Suppose you have a dog, and three different groups of people from different countries and who speak different languages are giving their account about the nature and character of a dog.

The English-speaking group says *dog* is a loyal animal, barks and wags his tail, etc.

The Spanish-speaking group says *perro* is a loyal animal, barks and wags his tail, etc.

The Farsi-speaking group says *sag* is a very loyal animal, barks and wags his tail, etc.

These three diverse groups use three different words (or names) for this creature (a linguistic issue). Looking at the nature and characteristics that they put forth—that is, the loyalty of the animal, the barking and wagging of the tail, etc.—we deduce that they all point to the same creature.

Put another way, if the Farsi-speaking people still called this creature *sag* but they said sag meows (doesn't bark) and it is not loyal, etc., then, this group and the English-speaking group are *not* describing the same creature.

Let's look at a person example.

Example 2: Suppose there are two books written about President Obama by two different people from different cultures. These books are written in different languages and may have been written in different times of Mr. Obama's adult life.

The first book describes him as a democrat, family-oriented, generous man who would never compromise his integrity, lie, or cheat. The writer further describes him as a man who loves people, is opposed to capital punishment, and is an involved parent.

The second book describes him as a republican and a very stingy man, who hates people, lies and cheats often, and is in favor of capital punishment. He also is described as a parent who is not involved with his children and an angry and aggressive man.

These two books either refer to two different people (maybe the same name), or if they both claim to describe the same President Obama, then one must be lying.

Since lying about the characteristics of a person can easily be disputed and false claims can be rejected, the most likely reason for the discrepancies is that the books are written about two different persons.

No matter how anyone feels about Mr. Obama, the fact is that he is either a democrat or a republican; he is either for capital punishment or against; he is either loving, generous, and honest or angry, aggressive, a liar, and a cheater.

I understand that we human beings sometimes demonstrate a bit of each opposite characteristic, but in general, we demonstrate a set of characteristics that are consistent and serve as our signature in the course of our lives.

Example 3: Suppose President Obama himself writes two books in two different languages—English and Swahili. He writes about himself, his desires, his habits, his likes and dislikes, his children, and his country. Also suppose these two books are written in different periods of his life.

Book #1. The Kenyan people who read his book in Swahili read the following:

- Barack Obama is a son of a white mother and a black Kenyan father.
- He changes his mind as he pleases and thus gives no assurance to his family or friends where he stands on an issue at any time.
- He has two children and lives in Washington DC.
- He hates people unless they do things his way.
- He is a democrat, supports abortion, and supports capital punishment
- He hates homosexuals, unwed mothers, non-Christians, and especially Jews.

Book #2. The American readers who read his other book in English a few years later find that:

- Barack Obama is a son of a white mother and a black father from the United States.
- His word is final, and he does not change his mind. Once he is a friend, you can count on him to be a friend always.
- He has two children and lives in Texas.
- He loves people and gives everyone a freedom to love him or not.
- He loves homosexuals, unwed mothers, all non-Christians, including Jews, Arabs, etc., although he may not agree with their lifestyle practices.

From the above example, any reasonable person can testify that one of these books does not represent Barack Obama, the president of the United States, because his description, character, and words, written by himself, are different when the two books are compared, and the linguistic nature of these books has nothing to do with this difference. The difference is about the character and nature of the person being portrayed. One of the books must be false.

So we conclude that either:

- These two books were not written by the same Barack Obama.
- These books are not about the same Barack Obama (two different people, same name).
- If other people wrote these books from President Obama's perspective, then one of the writers clearly changed some of the facts and character information for some personal reasons. This writer had a motive to change the truth! He stands to benefit from the lies and the deception and the falsehood.

When it comes to a holy God, however, the characteristics are everlasting, unchanging, and absolute, so identifying the differences between Allah and the God of the Bible is absolutely clear. There are no gray areas as there are in human beings.

Back to the critical question at hand: Is Allah just another name for the God of the Bible—YAWH—or is he a different person/god?

Regardless of what any group of people thinks, the attributes, deeds, and principles of these two references have to be the same, if they indeed point to the same entity. This is evaluated not based on what their followers, prophets, or even follower's practices may say (since that can be subjective) but based on the written word associated with each of these two names—that is, it is based on the Qur'an and the Holy Bible.

The following table lists a few intrinsic characteristics of God of the Bible and Allah. The contrast is inescapable as well as undeniable!

Holy Bible	Qur'an
1. YHWH never lies or deceives and cannot accept those who deceive. He is the truth (Ps 107:7, John 14:6, Titus 1:2)!	Allah admits that he deceives. In sureh 4:142 and 8:30, Allah refers to himself as "deceiver." In sureh 3:54, he calls himself "the best of schemers."
2. God is a triune being—one God in three persons—God the Father, God the Son, and God the Holy Spirit. "Go . . . and make disciples of all nations, baptizing them in the name of the Father and the Son, and the Holy Spirit" (Matt. 28:19-20). (See also John 1:1-2, John 5:26-27, Gal 1:1, Matt 3:16-17, Matt 28:19-20.)	Allah is *not* triune. Not only is he not a triune entity, but the Qur'an calls this doctrine a grave blasphemy (Q 5:72-73): "They do blaspheme who say; 'Allah is one of the three in a Trinity: for there is no god except one God." Q 4:171 says, "Do not say Trinity. Cease from doing that." (See also Q 5:17, 5:72,73,75)
3. God does not change. "For I AM the LORD, I change not" (Mal. 3:6). (See also James 1:17.)	Allah changes. "If We supersede any verse or cause it to be forgotten, We bring a better one or one similar" (Q 2:106).
4. God commands us *not* to kill. "Thou shall not kill" (Ex. 20:13).	Allah commands his followers to kill enemies. "Seize them and slay them wherever you find them" (Q 4:89).
5. God says, "Love your enemies" (Matt. 5:44, Luke 6:27-28).	

6. God has a Son. "This is my Son, whom I love; with him I am well pleased" (Luke 3:22, Matt 3:17, Mark 1:11). "God so Loved the world that He gave His only begotten Son ... " (John 3:16).	Allah does not have a son (Q 19:88). "He (Allah) begotten not, nor is he begotten" (Q 112).
7. God has an *exact* representation. Jesus says, "If you have seen me, you have seen the Father" (John 14:9).	Allah does not have an exact representation. "There is none like unto him (Allah)" (sureh 112).
8. God loves sinners. "It is because of these that I have come" (Matt 9:13). "While we were still sinners, Christ died for us" (Rom 5:8).	Allah hates sinners (Q 2:276, Q3:32 and 57, Q2:190). "For Allah loves not those who do wrong" (3:57). "I will fill Hell with demons and men all together" (sureh 32:13).
9. God loves *all* the people of the world—Jews, Gentiles (i.e., all non-Jews), male, female (John 3:16).	Allah hates all who are not Muslim, and he hates them so much that he commands them to be killed (sureh 9:29). See also Q 32:13 "I will fill Hell with demons and men all together."
10. Jews are special people of YHWH. He loves them with everlasting love. (Psalm 135:4, Deut 7:6, 2 Chro 20:7)	Allah holds Jews in contempt and commands Muslims not to take them as friend and fight and slay them. (Q 5:51, 5:82, 9:29, 98:6)

Moreover, there are ninety-nine names (or nicknames) for Allah that are reported in Islamic traditions and in Hadith, but none is YHWH or I AM, the actual names of the God of Jews and Christians.

As I said earlier, if Allah and the God of the Bible were the same being, they must possess the same characteristics and the same nature, and their message or commands must be consistent, not contradictory.

Allah may be an Arabic word for God, but it does not refer to the same God Christians and Jews worship, and since there is only one true God, then Allah must be a false god. Purposefully disregarding the clear distinction mentioned above would lead to a gross and "fatal" misrepresentation of the ultimate truth.

Hindus and many other religions also have names for God, and they refer to them as their god, but by looking at the character and nature of those gods, we can see that none are the same being as YHWH.

Taking a 100 percent pure truth, and smearing it to one's liking, which causes the truth to be less truthful than before, perhaps 70 percent or anything less than the original 100 percent, is presenting a falsehood. Depending of what the pure truth is, this smearing may not have grave consequences and thus may not be noticeable or an issue for people, but in the case of the ultimate truth and one's eternal salvation, this act would have a fatal and eternal consequence! Satan knows this very well.

Some time ago I came across a friend of mine who told me what someone very close to me said about my character to her and to others. She had portrayed me totally differently (in some instances as the opposite) than the way I really am. I heard that she even changed my words intentionally. But because other people didn't know me, they believed everything and were deceived. So this close person (who had her own agenda and reasons for what she was doing) used the same person (me) and some of the truth but twisted it, changed it, and portrayed a totally different person to her friends so they could sympathize with her and dislike me.

Now imagine if this distortion of truth is about the truth of life, and imagine if the one people dislike or deny is God Almighty, and imagine the person who does the distortion is Satan, and his agenda and reasons are to have as many souls in hell as possible.

Clearly, in the light of the evidence above, these two beings are not the same person. In fact, these two beings are so different that they are in the extreme opposite of each other! Allah is a different god with a drastically different nature and extremely different agenda than the God of Christians and Jews! Allah does not possess the nature of the God of Jews and Christians. Moreover, Allah lacks the love, the goodness, and the un-changeability that everyone, including Muslims, associates with the true God. Allah is a false god.

Remember that readers who want to know these facts can easily find them. The age of information has provided us with almost unlimited resources to research and find the truth. The only obstacle to this is the

Islamic leaders, governments, or even parents who censor information and use fear, intimidation, or legal grounds to prevent people from discovering the truth. To these people, I simply suggest from my own personal experience, that you need to seek the help of the true God and ask Him to reveal Himself and His truth to you in the privacy of your own home. Ask Him to help you light the way to the truth, and He will do just that. He has promised us this in His Word:

> *Ask and it will be given to you. Seek, and you shall find; knock and the door shall be open to you.*
> —Matthew 7:7

II. Mohammed—a False Prophet

If Mohammed is Allah's prophet, and in the above section, we found out that Allah is a false god, then logically, Mohammed is a false prophet.

But I wanted to prove this falsehood independent from the above finding.

Throughout history, God called certain individuals to proclaim His message of truth to people. Embedded in His truth is His plan for delivering His fallen people.

His plan was initiated by declaring to Satan:

> *And I will put enmity between you and the woman, and between your offspring and hers: he will crush your head, and you will strike his heel.*
> —Genesis 3:15

Let's look at several prophets who were called to advance God's truth and plan.

Abraham

In Christianity, Abraham is not considered one of the prophets but a friend of God. I include him here because Islam regards him as one and also because God called him to initiate the implementation of His plan for the Promised Land and for His special people who came to be known as Israelites. The Bible refers to Abraham as God's friend. God called

Abraham (Abram at the time) to leave his home country of Ur to the place that the Lord would give him, and that He would make him into a great nation, and his offspring would be as numerous as the stars of the sky.

He promised Abraham that he would have a son. Abraham and Sarah were in their eighties when God promised a son to them. Sarah was barren all her life. God picked a seemingly impossible situation to promise countless descendents and a great nation out of Abraham. Abraham, although from a pagan family and culture, found favor with God because he had an open and obedient heart and trusted in the invisible God.

Abram believed the Lord, and he credited it to him as righteousness.
—Genesis 15:6

God made a covenant with Abraham and told him that his descendents would be strangers in a country, and they would be enslaved and mistreated for four hundred years (Gen 15:13).

God gave to Abraham the land of Canaan (present Israel), and He said to Abraham:

And the LORD said to Abram, after Lot had separated from him, "Lift up your eyes from where you are and look north and south, east and west. All the land that you see I will give you and your offspring forever . . . Go walk through the length and breadth of the land, for I am giving it to you."
—Genesis 13:15

Twenty years passed and there was no child. Sarah's patience ran out. With the agreement of Abraham, Sarah decided to "fix" the childlessness problem and to help the coming of the promise of God, and she gave her Egyptian slave maiden to her husband, and she conceived Ishmael.

God reminded Abraham and Sarah of His promise and the fact that the promised child was going to be out of his seed and Sarah's seed. God repeated His covenant with Abraham:

Your wife Sarah will bear you a son, and you will call him Isaac. I will establish my covenant with him as an everlasting covenant for his descendants after him.
—Genesis 17:19

Finally God's promise came to fruition, and Isaac was born. Isaac (not Ishmael) was a part of God's plan.

> *But my covenant will I establish with Isaac, which Sarah shall bear unto thee at this time in the next year.*
> —Genesis 17:21

God manifested His power, sovereignty, faithfulness, and love through His testing of Abraham. He asked him to sacrifice his son, his only son, Isaac on the Mount Moriah.

> *Then God said, "Take your son, your only son, Isaac, whom you love, and go to the region of Moriah. Sacrifice him there as a burnt offering on one of the mountains I will tell you about."*
> —Genesis 22:2

On their way to the mountain, Isaac asked his father, ""The fire and the wood are here," Isaac said, "but where is the lamb for the burnt offering?" Abraham answered, "God himself will provide the lamb for the burnt offering, my son" (Gen 22:8).

Later, as Abraham lifted his hand with the knife to sacrifice his son for God, the angel of God stopped him and told him not to kill his son and that he had shown his faithfulness. God provided a lamb in a bush for the sacrifice.

This was to show that God's plan was for Isaac to be born, to live, and to have a son named Jacob, whom God would later renamed Israel. Jacob's son Joseph, who became a great leader in Egypt, ended up saving his family and extended family, altogether about seventy people, from famine by bringing them into Egypt. These Israelites later would be slaves in Egypt for four hundred years, just as God told Abraham.

Moses

Moses, a Levi Hebrew, was born in slavery in Egypt during Pharaoh's reign. Pharaoh ordered every male Hebrew son to be thrown into the Nile River. Moses' mother put him in a basket and set him out on the bank of the river with his sister watching from a distance. Pharaoh's daughter found him and adopted him. Moses grew up as a prince in the house of Pharaoh but had compassion toward his own people. He defended one of the Hebrew slaves by killing his Egyptian master, and for that, he had to leave Egypt into wilderness and later reached Midian near Sinai.

Soon Moses was called by God to deliver His people (now about two million of them) from Egypt. God introduced Himself at Mount Sinai, "I am the God of your fathers, the God of Abraham, the God of Isaac and the God of Jacob" (Ex 3:6).

In verse 10, God told Moses of His plan: "Therefore come now and I will send you to Pharaoh, so that you may bring My people, the sons of Israel, out of Egypt." Moses asked, "When people asked me who sent me what shall I say?" (Ex 3:14). God answered, "Tell them, I AM sent you."

Moses knew well who I AM was, what was His plan was, and what His attributes were. Moses, the Israelites, and even pagans saw the glimpse of God's plan during the Exodus. Moses empowered by God, performed great miracles that brought plagues over Egypt. The last plague was the death of all firstborn of Egypt, which finally caused Pharaoh to free the people of Israel. The Passover marked the first deliverance of the people through a lamb's shed blood brushed on the doorframes of the Israelites' homes.

This event, although known to God Himself at the time, pointed also to the future when the final Deliverer, the one and only Lamb of God, would come, and His blood would be shed for the sins of the people.

Moses later brought the Ten Commandments, inscribed by the finger of God, to the people and told them to trust in the one and only God—YHWH. These commandments are called the Law or Testimony and reveal God's standard of living for people. The Law also demonstrates people's incapability to adhere to it and thus their sinful nature.

EZRA

Ezra was a priest and teacher of the Law. He led a group of exiled Jews back to the Promised Land and helped them rebuild the temple of God and taught them the proper way of worship. Not one line of the Law or Scripture of Moses was changed. He was another spokesman for God.

ISAIAH

Isaiah is one of my favorite prophets. He was called by God to prophesy to Judah (Isa 1:1). He prophesied the coming of the Messiah seven hundred years before the Messiah came!

> For unto us a child is born, to us a son is given, and the government will be on his shoulder. And he will be called Wonderful Counselor, Almighty God Everlasting Father, Prince of Peace. Of the increase of his government and peace there will be no end. He will reign on David's throne and over his kingdom, establishing and upholding it with justice and righteousness from that time on and forever (Isa 9:6-7).

Again, seven hundred years before Jesus came to earth, Isaiah prophesied the Messiah's death on the cross. Execution by crucifixion did not even exist in Isaiah's time! He wrote, "But he was pierced for our transgressions He was crushed for our iniquities; the punishment that brought us peace was upon him, and by his wounds we are healed" (Isa 53:5). He also prophesied in Isaiah 53:12, "Because he poured out his life unto death, and was numbered with the transgressors for he bore the sin of many and made intercession for the transgressors."

EZEKIEL

Ezekiel was called to bring to Israelites, who were in exile in Babylon, a message of hope and deliverance (Eze1:3). He had many visions and prophesies from the Lord. Some of these visions have already come true. Some are still in the future.

He prophesied that the Israelites in exile would all be gathered in the Promised Land and united and would establish a nation. This prophecy came to fruition in 1948, the formal establishment of the state of Israel.

In Ezekiel 37:24, he prophesied that, "My servant David will be king over them, and they will all have one shepherd."

Hundreds of years later, David (*Davoud* in Farsi), a small shepherd, miraculously fought and killed the Philistine giant Goliath, and later he became the king of Israel, just as Ezekiel prophesied.

DANIEL

Prophet Daniel, who God called out of Jewish exile, was put in the Lion's den (Dan 6) by the Persian pagan king Nebuchadnezzar, but God delivered him. The king put him in charge of his kingdom. Later, King Darius of Persia gave this order:

> I issue a decree that in every part of my kingdom people must fear and reverence the God of Daniel. For He is the living God; And He endures forever; His kingdom will never end. He rescues and He saves; He performs signs and wonders in the heavens and on the earth. He has rescued Daniel from the power of the lions (Dan 6:25-27).

None of the prophets listed above changed, denied, or twisted even one line of the Scriptures or the history of Abraham, his sons, Noah and his family, the nature of God, and/or the plan of God.

Finally, God's plan to redeem His people by bringing about the only Redeemer, the Deliverer, the Messiah and Savior of the world was executed by the birth of Jesus in Bethlehem. His earthly lineage was from the Hebrew tribe of Judah, just as the prophet Isaiah foretold seven hundred years before.

Messiah Jesus

Jesus was the Incarnate Word of God who came down from heaven (John 6:38) to rescue us. The people marveled at His words and His love. They called Him several names:

- The Carpenter (Mark 6:3)
- The Teacher (John 13:13)
- The Prophet (John 4:19, 7:40)
- The Rabbi (John 4:31, 9:2)
- The Son of Man (John 9:35)

He was all of above and more—much more. He was and is:

- The Son of God (John 1:34, 1:49, Luke 22:70, Mark 15:39)
- The Redeemer (Isa 60:16)
- The Lord (John 11:12)

- The Word of God (John 1:1)
- The Resurrection (John 11:25)
- The Way, the Truth, and the Life (John 14:6)
- The Light of the world (John 8:12)
- The Bread of Life (John 6:35, 48)
- The Living Water (John 4:13)
- The Lamb of God (John 1:29)
- The Good Shepherd (John 10:11, 14)
- The Christ (John 11:27, Luke 2:11, 24:44)
- The Messiah (Dan 9:25)
- The Savior (Luke 2:11)
- The Wonderful Counselor (Isa. 9:6)
- Emanuel—God with us (Matt 1:23)
- The Prince of Peace (Isa 9:6)
- The Bright Morning Star (Rev 22:16)
- The King (John 18:37)
- The Alpha and Omega (Rev 22:13)
- The First and the Last, the Beginning and the End (Rev 22:13)
- The I AM (John 8:58)

Jesus, being the Son of God, never denied, changed, or rejected any part of the Law and the prophecies from the time of Adam to Abraham to His time. By referencing the written words of the prophets, He gave them validity. He fulfilled them. As a matter of fact, He said, "Do not think that I have come to abolish the Law or the Prophets; I have not come to abolish them, but to fulfill them" (Matt 5:17).

God's plan, message, and character, the people He used, and His prophets' words and deeds were all consistent and in agreement throughout the books of the Bible. They were threaded and weaved into each other throughout the span of thousands of years, as if with a visible, strong scarlet thread! There was no contradiction or elimination, no change in the content and nature or plans of God. No change in God's character or Word ever occurs throughout the Bible.

Now let's see what is in that scarlet *thread* that is able to bind together these prophets and the Messiah who lived in different time periods through the span of four thousand years.

Here are some common elements between all these prophets and even those in the Holy Bible that are not mentioned here, such as Joel, Amos, and Micah:

1. All the prophets are Jews. God's plan for the world revolves around and is through His chosen people of Israel. Throughout the Bible, God chose a son from the twelve tribes of Israel in every generation to put forth his plan of bringing the Messiah to the world stage for the redemption of mankind.
2. In Deuteronomy 18:18, the Lord says, "I will raise up for them a prophet like you among their brothers. I will put my words in their mouth." This verse clarifies that God sent the prophets from "among brothers" who were Jews. Also, that's why Jesus said to the Pharisee woman that, "the salvation is from the Jews" (John 4:22). In other words, the salvation of mankind will come out of the Jews.
3. All the prophets performed miracles, by the power of God, to show that God has empowered them to be His spokesmen.
4. All of the prophets foretold the future, not of their own power but by the power of God's Spirit.
5. The prophets mentioned above never contradicted, changed, or denied the plan, words, deeds, or character of God or the previous prophets.

The atonement of sin is completed, and there is no need for any prophet. Through Jesus, God the Father has now given each believer, great or small, rich or poor, man or woman, Jew or Gentile, direct access to His throne (Eph 2:18)!

Once the thread is pulled to the end, we see Jesus, the Messiah whose coming was prophesied in the Holy Bible by all the above prophets, saying that He will be killed for the sins of the world, and on the third day, He will be raised.

At the cross, He gave up His last breath and uttered these words: "It is finished" (John 19:30).

God's plan for rescuing mankind was finished at the cross by the blood of Jesus shed for anyone who puts his trust in Him. The work of atonement for sin was completed and accepted by the Father. The resurrection of Christ proved the acceptance and also marked the victory over sin and death.

Now that we looked at the content of the *tread*—that is, the common elements of the true prophets of God—let's measure Mohammed against the revealed commonalities.

Evidence for Falsehood of Mohammed as a Prophet

Let us now compare these common factors of prophets with Mohammed:

1. Mohammed was not a Jew and was outside of God's plan. Therefore, he couldn't have been a true prophet from the Lord.
2. He changed the character of God (see the previous discussion in this chapter). He rejected God's triune nature. He rejected Jesus as the Son of God. He rejected Jesus' deity and Lordship. He changed the story of Isaac and Ishmael by saying that it was Ishmael who was about to be sacrificed. He changed the account of Noah's wife from that of the Holy Bible. He changed God's method of paying for sins—not through blood but through good works. He rejected the crucifixion of Jesus. If h changed God's plan, he cannot be from God.
3. He denied the resurrection of Jesus from the dead.
4. He claimed to be the "seal of prophets" and greater than all the prophets, including Jesus, along with rejecting, denying, or changing critical doctrines in Judaism and Christianity, yet he left nothing other than a call for jihad or set nothing more than an example of "kill or convert" for his people.
5. He never prophesied about the future.
6. He never performed miracles, either of his own power or by the power of God.
7. Mohammed himself did not believe the voice he heard in the cave was from God. In fact, he thought he was possessed by the devil. It was his wife who convinced him that he was a prophet

and it was God's angel who spoke to him, even though she was not with him to see or hear anything.

8. Mohammed did not bring any atonement of sin to be the seal of prophets or to bring the last, best, and most complete revelation of God!
9. Mohammed, as opposed to all the previous prophets (who, by the way, are accepted by Islam), used war, killing, and violence to establish his religion.
10. Mohammed, as opposed to all the previous prophets, exalted himself to the level of Allah, his god. To show allegiance to Allah, one must pray that Allah is god and Mohammed is his apostle (sureh 48:8-9, 3:32, 9:80, 9:29, etc.). The link of Allah and Mohammed is a part of the confession of faith, *"Shohada,"* and all other prayer verses. Without Allah, a Muslim cannot have Mohammed, and without Mohammed, he cannot have Allah. To be a Muslim, a belief in Allah and Mohammed as his prophet is essential. Mohammed has made himself equal to his god.
11. Mohammed, unlike all the previous prophets, produced no good fruit but instilled in his followers hatred for followers of Moses and Jesus. In Islam, Moses and Jesus are respected and validated as Messengers of God, the Torah and the Bible are called, the Book, which is truth, and the followers are called, "The people of the Book" (Q4:171). Yet he slaughtered the Jews of his time and told his followers to kill the Jews and Christians. He taught the "kill or convert" method to his people to bring as many people under his religion as possible. Bad fruit cannot come from a true prophet (Matt 7:15-19).
12. He elevated the status of men over women. He is recorded in Hadith as saying, "I was shown the Hell-fire and the majority of its dwellers are women." To date, in an Islamic court such as in Iran, the witness of two women is necessary to counter the witness of one man (Q 2:282). This is ungodly act for a prophet.

Watch out for false prophets. They come to you in sheep's clothing, but inwardly they are ferocious wolves. By their fruit you will recognize them. Do people pick grapes from thorn bushes, or figs from thistles?

Likewise, every good tree bears good fruit; but a bad tree bears bad fruit. A good tree cannot bear bad fruit, nor can a bad tree bear good fruit.
—Matthew 7:15-19

Mohammed may be a real prophet of Allah, but he is a false prophet as far as the true God is concerned.

III. Qur'an—a False Doctrine

Islam Denies the Deity of Jesus

Another piece of evidence for the purposeful deception is how Islam's Qur'an insists on misrepresenting the biblical Jesus despite six hundred-plus years of written manuscripts about Him by the time Islam came along. The Qur'an, Satan's campaign tool, denies Jesus' deity (because it puts Him above Mohammed), denies His crucifixion (because it provides for the atonement of sin and thus it eliminates the very need for Islam), and denies His resurrection (because it shows the way for salvation, the victory of Jesus [and those of us who put our faith in Him] over sin, and therefore there is no need for Islam). Let's look at each of these core elements of Christianity and Jesus' purpose on earth.

1. His Unique Birth

Look at the following verse from the Qur'an:

When angel said, "O Mary! Verily God announced to thee the Word from Him: His name shall be Messiah Jesus . . . she said, 'How O my Lord! Shall I have a son, when man has not touched me?' He said, 'Thus: God will create what He will'" (Q: 3:45-47).

a. The *Virgin* Mary. No one in the history of mankind has ever been impregnated and given birth while being a virgin. This in itself is supernatural, and the Qur'an records it.

b. The announcer is an angel. This, by anyone's standard, especially the Islamic world, is an extraordinary event orchestrated only by God.

c. The angel said, "Verily God announced to thee the Word from Him." The Bible says, "In the beginning was the Word, and the Word was with God and the Word was God . . . and the Word became flesh and dwelled among us, and we beheld His glory, the glory as of the only begotten of the Father, full of grace and truth" (John 1:1, 14). The Qur'an refers to Jesus as the Word of God; with a little analysis and thoughtful consideration, every Muslim can come to the conclusion that the Word of God is not a creation of God but is of God Himself.
d. The Qur'an says, "His name shall be Messiah Jesus . . ." The Messiah is the Deliverer. The Messiah was to come to deliver mankind from the bondage of sin. Even the Qur'an itself does not give this title to Mohammad, who claimed to be the seal of prophets.
e. When Mary answers, "How O my Lord shall I have a son, when man has not touched me?" God answers, "God will create what He will." The Qur'an acknowledges that God is able to father the child that is going to be conceived in Mary's womb without any "man" involved.

Sureh 19:17 states: "We [God] sent our spirit to her [Mary], and he [Jesus] took before her the form of a perfect man." The Qur'an states that God sent His Spirit to Mary, and Jesus took the form of a perfect man!

First: God's Spirit is upon Mary

The Qur'an records that the Spirit of God came upon the Virgin Mary, and she conceived, yet it refers to Him only as the son of Mary and not the Son of God. Especially in a paternal society such as Arabia (and the greater Middle East), a son is identified by who his father is rather than by who his mother is. The insistence of Islam in repeatedly referring to Jesus as the son of Mary shows two things: 1. That Islam goes out of its way to identify Jesus with Mary because it cannot identify any man for the father. 2. Islam is trying to avoid and deny the truth that Jesus is the Son of God!

In Iran, when marriages between the Iranian women and American men became more common, people in Iran referred to the children as Americans because the father was from America. Even to this day, in the event of a divorce, the children are automatically given to the father unless the wife can prove he is either in prison for life, addicted to drugs, or has abandoned the children.

So for the Qur'an to practically dismiss its own account that the "spirit of God came upon Virgin Mary and she conceived" and repeatedly call Jesus the son of Mary only, and never refer to Him as the Son of God is indicative of a intentional, malicious act to deceive, misrepresent, and deny the significance of this unique birth and supernatural being.

Second: He Took the Form of . . .

Then Jesus "took the form of . . ." This implies that He was not in the "form of" before this event. He was not in the form of a man before.

Third: . . . a Perfect Man

"The form of a perfect man." We all know that no human being is perfect unless He is more than a man! Islam believes that only God is perfect. Using the Qur'an own account, Jesus *must* be God. The Qur'an does not like to admit to this obvious and logical truth.

Fourth: Sinless Jesus

Sureh 19:19 of the Qur'an acknowledges the sinless nature of Jesus. Sinlessness is a characteristic that no human being in history in the history of mankind has ever had or claimed to posses, yet the Qur'an calls Jesus a prophet only. He was sinless because He was more than a prophet and more than a human being because He was more than a son of Mary; He was sinless because He was God! He is God with us, Emmanuel!

2. Crucifixion

Although as a Muslim I had heard from outside sources that Jesus (*Isa*) was crucified (the Qur'an rejects this), I believed that it was a cruel way of execution and that was the way executions were carried out two thousand years ago.

No one told us about the wages of sin, the deity of Jesus, the story of the cross, the empty tomb, the resurrection, and the redemption. The most critical, life-and-death information that affects every single human being in the history of mankind was intentionally hidden from us.

How is it possible that the Qur'an denies His crucifixion despite a great number of historical accounts that had covered this event in history, since it turned out that it was not an ordinary crucifixion carried out by the Romans and some other cultures two thousand years ago? At this crucifixion, the earth trembled, the sky darkened, the veil of Holy of Holies in the temple of Jerusalem tore, and even His enemies came to believe that indeed, "He was truly the Son of God" (Mark 15:39).

The Qur'an changes the story and says that some other person was crucified in place of Him (Q 4:157).

3. Resurrection

How is it possible that the Qur'an does not even mention the greatest event in human history—the resurrection?

Sureh 4:158 says that Jesus was raised to God without death.

The purpose was to deceive. Satan did what he does best; he took the truth and twisted it for his purpose—a good prophet instead of the Messiah, another one crucified instead of the Jesus Christ, son of Mary instead of the Son of God, raised to God without death, instead of resurrected from the dead.

Islam knowingly and maliciously, despite all the historical evidence available in the seventh century and beyond, denies the deity of Jesus, His death on the cross, and His resurrection from the dead. Thus, it is an anti-Christ religion.

> *But every spirit that does not acknowledge Jesus, is not from God. This is the spirit of the antichrist which you have heard is coming and even now is already in the world.*
> *—1 John 4:3*

> *Many deceivers, who do not acknowledge Jesus Christ as coming in the flesh, have gone out into the world. Any such person is the deceiver and the antichrist.*
> *—2 John 1:7*

Islam is Satan's tool, deliberately and purposefully designed to undermine the work and the plan of God by deceiving people and hiding from them the fact that Jesus is the only way to salvation and eternal life.

More Evidence for Purposeful Deception

1. Prohibition on questioning or criticizing the Qur'an, Allah, or Mohammed. The violation of this prohibition results in death!
2. Translation issues. Islamic leaders state that the Qur'an cannot be understood in any language other than Arabic. Most Arabs, who do not understand it even in their native language, justify it by claiming that the Qur'an is beyond any human's understanding. It was only in the last century that non-Arab scholars who have learned Arabic began to translate it, and now, infused with the information age and its Internet and social media, the Qur'an is exposed and naked! It is incoherent, inconsistent, and full of confusion, contradictions, and in some areas, a total nonsense.
3. There is a death sentence for those who leave Islam to follow other religions.
4. There is a death sentence for those who speak to Muslims about Jesus Christ.
5. It changes God's Word on the story of Abraham and Isaac (Q 37:100), the flood (Q 11:42-43), Jesus' birth and crucifixion (Barnabas was crucified instead of Jesus, Q 4:157), and the resurrection (Q 4:158). Satan's agenda is clear. He wants to smear the truth to portray that Jesus was not sacrificed for the sins of mankind and was not resurrected because that fact is what causes people to draw to Him and to be saved.
6. If one asks Muslims how they think of Jesus, they say they accept and respect Him, just as they accept and respect Moses. But the Qur'an repeatedly calls for the killing of all Christians and Jews (Q 2:191, 9:29, 3:85, 4:89, 8:13-17). Both Moses and Jesus were Jews; Jesus Christ was the fulfillment of God's promises in Torah. So how could they (or Allah) be against Christians and

Jews, yet accept and respect these two prophets? The doctrine seems to be illogical at best.

7. Islam says that Islam is superior to Christianity and Judaism and that is why Allah sent Mohammed to be the final prophet for the most complete, ultimate religion. He did this because the Jews and Christians corrupted the Books (and therefore the truth) and changed them to the point that they are no longer true.

    This tells us that Islam believes Allah was not able to protect his word from corruption, and in other words, he failed, twice, and thus made the third move with Mohammed! This tells us that Islam believes people have more power (even if evil) than Allah!

8. Back to "respecting" Jesus. The Bible quotes Jesus as saying, "Before Abraham was, I AM" (John 8:58). The phrase, "I AM" is God's name that was given to Moses on Mount Sinai by the burning bush when Moses asked God, "What should I tell them when they ask me who sent you?" and God replied, "Tell them I AM sent you."

    Jesus was telling the Jewish priests that He is the great I AM, God incarnate! Since it is blasphemous for any man to equate himself with God, the priests went after Jesus on this charge and had Him crucified. Later, all believed He was more than a man, more than a good teacher or a prophet, because when Jesus died on the cross, all hell broke loose! The sun darkened, the earth shook, and at the temple, the Jewish priests' nightmare occurred—the veil of the Holy of Holies tore from the top to bottom!

    Islam, too, believes that Jesus was just a man. So, in other words, Jesus either lied when He claimed He was God or He was a crazy man who thought he was God. How is it possible that Islam (with the perfection it attempts to portray) respects a crazy man or a liar as a prophet? This is obviously a false doctrine.

By this you know the Spirit of God: Every spirit that confesses that Jesus Christ has come in the flesh is of God, and every

> *spirit that does not confess that Jesus Christ has come in the flesh is not of God. And this spirit is of the Antichrist, which you have heard was coming, and is now already in the world.*
>
> —1 John 4:2-3

A chill moved over my skin. I could see the hairs on my arms standing up in utter shock and shame. I had been worshipping a false god without knowing it. Only when I found the truth and believed in the one and only Savior of the world did I realize that for most of my life, I had been living in a world of lies and deceit, had been an accomplice to the works of Satan unknowingly, and was an enemy of the one who was hung on the cross for me and because of me, all so I could be set free.

The light of truth exposed the darkness and all it contained. My Savior said it well in His eternal Word: *"I am the light of the world. Whoever follows me will never walk in darkness, but will have the light of life"* (John 8:12).

I spent hours in prayer and communion with my Savior over this. I needed His guidance, His Spirit of love and forgiveness to overshadow me. I needed protection for my heart and my mind from any ill thoughts or desires for my betrayers. I prayed fervently with tears for strength and the desire to forgive. I needed to look at them the way Jesus looked at His enemies at the cross, still with love, and asked the Father to forgive them. I needed to love like Jesus did more than anything at this time. Anything short of that, I knew, would leave me bitter, angry, and captive.

My prayers were answered almost immediately. It was God's grace that compelled me to not wish my betrayers any ill but to want the same new life for them. I forgave the false prophet, the teachers, the family members, and all the Islamic teachers, leaders, and accomplices who led and promoted this incredible betrayal of people. I could not have imagined, just months ago, forgiving these countless lies and deceptions, but now that I was covered with God's grace, I had no other desire but to see them forgiven and at the feet of Jesus! His grace is sufficient for all and is sufficient forever. His grace is like a boundless, rushing river of life flowing through the hearts and souls of those who call on Him.

I discovered that if one is conquered by love, one is able to conquer the sting of betrayals, abuse, and shame. I was conquered by the precious blood of the one who came as the tangible, physical expression of YHWH's core essence—love.

> *Love is patient; love is kind ... it keeps no records of wrongdoings ... Love never fails.*
> —1 Corinthians 13:4-8

With Jesus, I never fail.

7

Showers of Blessings

*You are the God who performs miracles; You
display your power among the peoples.*

—*Psalm 77:14*

My father died in Iran on October 23, 1990. This was the same day fifteen years earlier that I married my German-American husband despite my father's strong opposition. His love for me was more than the strength of his opposition. He came to Isfahan, where I lived, to be a witness and to sign the marriage documents as my father. His fatherly love, compassion, and faithfulness often remind me of my Father in heaven, for He has been continuously compassionate and faithful despite my early difficult Christian living.

Paid in Full

I was living alone and in separation from my husband. I was taking care of my two small children, going through a contested divorce, had a new job in a new state with no family or friends, and had over $20,000 in debt. The debts were my father's hospital bills, pharmacy bills, a few doctors' bills, and his return ticket loan, and I also had some student loans of my own. My children suffered a lot, but I was determined to give them the best childhood possible.

The only way to grieve the loss of my dear father was to call my mother and sister for several weeks. I was so focused on my own pain that I did not want to think about the cost of the calls. Back in the early '90s, calls to Iran were very expensive—around a dollar per minute. I called every other day and spoke and cried on the phone for over an hour each time. Once I came to myself and realized that I had called a lot, I reduced it to one call per week and after a few weeks to one call per month. I knew my bill should be in hundreds of dollars, and I had no idea what I would do. My mother and sister did not know anything about the high cost of long-distance calls or about my overall debt situation. They just wanted to be there for me when I needed to be comforted.

My first test in my new relationship with my Lord was now surrounding me from all sides. Like a little child who has just lost everything and is desperate for help, I looked up to heavens and prayed that my Helper would come to my rescue, just as my earthly father would have done, had he been there, and would see me through. As His Word declares, "God is faithful for He cannot deny Himself" (2 Tim 2:13).

He came to my rescue, for He could not deny Himself of being the rescuer of His children.

The phone bill came. At first, I was afraid of opening it. I had no money at all. Even the regular local phone bill was too difficult to afford, but when I made those calls following my father's death, I wasn't thinking about the bill. I only knew I had lost my beloved father who was everything to me and to the family.

I finally opened the bill. I looked for the few hundred dollars' worth of calls. I could only see the minimum local charges. There were no traces of the calls to Iran. I thought maybe it was due to the billing cycle, and so I waited for the month after.

The month after came, and the bill had no charges of calls to Iran. Months passed. After a year, I thought, *It will surely be included in the last bill of the year because that's when inventories are done and all the checks and balances occur.*

The last bill of the year came, and there were no charges. All my other calls were charged except my calls to Iran. I even called the phone company to see if there was anything I owed. I specifically asked them if there were long distance calls to Iran that had not been paid.

They checked. "No. Your bill is paid in full," the man said from the other end of the phone. They further said that there were no calls to Iran recorded in the past several months.

But I knew better. I broke down in tears because I knew that God had erased all the calls I had made while grieving the death of my father.

The lowly He sets on high, and those who mourn are lifted to safety.
—Job 5:11

He knew I couldn't pay. I was an infant in my new birth, yet I had a very clear and close relationship with my Savior. He paid my debt by wiping it off of my record, just as He did at Golgotha, the outskirts of Jerusalem, two thousand years ago!

The Return Ticket

During his visit to the United States in 1989, my father was not optimistic about recovering from his cancer. Deep down in his heart, he knew that the cancer was winning because he was getting weaker. His return ticket had a long layover in Frankfort. He wanted a ticket that got him to Iran in shortest possible time, so I borrowed some money from my bank and bought two new tickets. I planned to return the old tickets and perhaps get a small refund for the unused portion. Once my father went back and I moved to Virginia, I returned the unused portion to the airline and asked if any refund was due to me. I was still paying the loan to the bank, and any small refund would be helpful, I thought. I prayed that the airline would be kind and fair.

A couple of weeks later, I received a check for $350 and then received another for $350. I thought that was it. Two refunds for two tickets were not bad at all, and so I was happy that I received that much. My loan was $2,000, and anything toward it was a big help. But in the next several weeks, I received more checks. They all totaled $2,000! I called my lawyer to see if I could use them even though I thought they were more than the return trip value. He checked and called back and said that I could use them. I called the airline myself too and asked if the checks were made in error. They checked and said that I was entitled to all the checks for a total of $2,000. Because the checks were for the amount I borrowed, I knew it was the Lord's doing.

I was able to pay off my loan the following month. Again, I praised my one and only Savior who never forsakes me.

Healed by His Stripes at 4:00 a.m.

In 2003, there was an epidemic of flu that killed fourteen children in the United States and a few elderly people and left millions of sick people.

My little granddaughter, Lily, twenty-seven months old at the time, caught it too. She was dying of it. There was a shortage of vaccines, so there was a ration plan employed where only the elderly and the children under two were being vaccinated.

Since Lily was a few months past two years of age, she was not eligible, but all the hospitals in Florida were out of the vaccine anyway. We were on the verge of losing our Lily. They told my daughter they could not do anything for her child. They could not even bring down her fever. They also told my daughter that the Louisiana hospital had vaccines, but they didn't think Lily could make the eleven-hour trip that night. The hospital sent her home with the child.

My daughter called me and frantically told me how Lily was dying in front of her eyes. I told her to take her back to the hospital despite what they told her because at least there would be people there if she needed help, so she did.

Here in Virginia, I got on my knees and asked my Savior and the Great Physician for help. I recalled that His Word said, "By His stripes we are healed"! (Isa 53:5, 1 Pet 2:24).

Jesus had never let me down before. I went to bed that night with crying eyes, but with full expectation.

> *In the morning, O LORD, you hear my voice; in the morning*
> *I lay my requests before you and wait in expectation*
> —Psalm 5:3

Although my eyes were full of tears and I could tell I was too sensitive to even a thought of my grandchild, I was free from worry. I knew my Savior knew my situation and He was in control. I waited in expectation of Him!

I fell asleep. I dreamed Christ Jesus came to the room. The room was a foggy color, but I could see clearly His white robe. He came and slowly passed by me, and instantly I was filled with His peace and love. It was like blowing air into a balloon that is ready to burst! I woke up and was overwhelmed with His love and with calmness. I looked at the clock by my bed, and it was 4:00. I got up, took a deep breath, looked outside my living room, and again was overwhelmed with my dream, the presence of the Lord, and His peace. I drank some water and went back to sleep.

I woke up at 8:00. It was a workday. I had already planned to fly that evening to Florida. I called my daughter to see what went on the previous night and how Lily was doing.

She told me that she went to the hospital the night before, as I had asked her. They again explained to her there was nothing more they could do. They could not help my little Lily. A nurse told them that there was a private hospital for cancer children and that they might be able to bring down her fever! She said they went there. The nurses took Lily and put her in dry ice for some time. Then she continued, "They brought her back to me. She was looking at me and she looked well. It was 4:00, and we left."

When she mentioned 4:00, I suddenly remembered my dream and Jesus! I lost control of the phone. I lost control of my legs. I fell to the ground and started to praise Him for His intervention and for healing her. I recalled His eternal Word: "By His stripes we are healed" (1 Pet 2:24).

I was amazed not only that He healed her but that He also came to me to tell me, *"It is finished!"*

Now that she is older—nine years old and a believer herself—she tells her friends how God saved her life when she was only two years old. She once wrote in a note to her tooth fairy, "Tell God I love him and I always will believe in Him."

Every time she smiles, dances, plays piano, or just giggles, I know I owe it to His stripes! Every breath she takes is a reminder that she was left for dead by the doctors and the hospitals, but Jesus disagreed!

His love truly endures forever. Praise and glory be to His name.

Tech Support from the Great Engineer

During my first encounter with the writing power of the Holy Spirit back in 1990, He inspired and brought about the confession poem that led me to see and know the one and only true God. This caused me to realize that I have a Savior who wants to free me from captivity and from all strongholds that exist between my heavenly Father and me. After this, I knew whom I must go to if I had a writing need.

It was the early 2005, and I was working on my doctorate program. I was working full time and going to school for the past three years and was working on my systems engineering doctorate degree.

I had two months off from my work so I could finish my dissertation. During these two months, I also had a candidacy exam to complete. I had four complex and elaborate questions to answer. I looked at the first question. *I think I can do this,* I thought. The second one was doable too. But the third one—I had no clue. I took it to the Lord.

"Lord, I will do the first two and the last one, and You think about the third one because I have no clue!" Of course, I knew He didn't have to think about it!

I started with the first question, later did the second one, and then answered the last one. It took about an hour each to finish them. I got to the third one, and I knew the Lord had the answer. I started writing. My mind was full of already-prepared thoughts. I was ready to answer the question even though I remembered that I had no clue a few hours before. My pen was on fire! An hour later, I was done, or I should say, He was done! I looked at the answer and said, "Wow, Lord! This is good!"

Few months later, after my graduation, I had lunch with one of my advisors who I knew wasn't a believer in Jesus Christ. I don't recall how the conversation started, but she said, "And you did great on the candidacy exam too, especially the question number three!" I told her with great joy that the Lord helped me with that! She laughed and said, "Oh, OK. As long as you didn't have help from a human being!"

"The Life of Christ" in an Antique Shop

I love antique shops. I love looking for old books, old china, ceramics, or old crosses. I can easily spend a whole day going through a small antique shop!

One beautiful afternoon in the spring of 2005, I was driving from the Old Dominion University (ODU) in Norfolk back to King George. I had passed a little antique shop in the middle of a small town a hundred times. I had been driving this road for three years, passing by the store, and always desiring to see it, but I had never stopped. During those three years, I had been traveling to ODU for my doctorate program. My doctoral program was covered by the government so I always used a government car. Because the rules are that we cannot use the car for personal business, I never stopped to look at this shop.

However, on this particular afternoon, I was in my personal car. The program was completed, and I went to ODU to get copies of my dissertation. Now upon reaching this store, my face came to life, and I was smiling even before I parked the car.

As I walked to the shop, I was conversing with my Lord: "Lord, I want to find a beautiful, old, old Bible." I was smiling, and I knew He was smiling back. I walked toward the bookshelves that I saw on my right. I soon noticed that there were thousands of books, and they were not organized in any particular order! Old books were mixed with modern books, which were mixed with history books, which were mixed with Christian books, mixed with recipe books, etc. There was no way to find something good—even if I had the whole day.

So I took it to my Wonderful Counselor, and I whispered to Him, asking Him to direct me to a good old Bible or a book about Him. I asked my request quietly, because people were around and I didn't want them to think I was talking to myself.

Just as I finished speaking to the Lord, I stood up and walked away from the books. The Lord told me there wasn't any book there that I was interested in, so I walked away. The Lord directed me toward the furniture section right in front of the book section. Although looking at furniture wasn't why I stopped there, I didn't mind. I always liked looking at old furniture!

A beautiful bedroom dresser with a large and elegant mirror caught my attention. *Probably from a castle,* I thought. It looked like a dresser for a royalty!

The Lord took my attention away from the grandness of the dresser and instead directed my eyes a little lower, *on* the dresser. I saw an object there, but I couldn't see what it was. I walked slowly toward it with great excitement. I knew my Lord had something for me.

As I was getting closer, it seemed as if the whole place around it was fading away into a blur, and my total focus was on this small object on the dresser. I was already smiling, knowing that the Lord was giving me something. I was too anxious to see what it was. I got to the dresser and looked. It was an oversized book! It looked very old and beautiful. And its title was *The Life of Christ*!

I cried from joy, for the Lord had not only heard me but also directed me away from the books (where one expects a book to be) but to the most unusual place to find exactly what I wanted!

The book was written in 1875 and had a pencil mark price written: $10! This book is my treasure, not only because it is antique, poetic, and in eloquent, classic English about our Lord but also because the Lord Himself found it for me!

Here is an excerpt to show this unique book's eloquent, classic English observation in regard to our Lord's first miracle at a wedding:

> He came not to hush the natural music of men's lives nor to fill it with storm and agitation, but to re-tune every silver chord in that "harp of a thousand strings," and to make it echo with the harmonics of Heaven.

Happy Birthday, My Child!

It was November 2006. I was paying two mortgages because I had just moved into my new house and the old house was for sale. This is the year that the housing market began to deteriorate and eventually collapsed. It was almost six months into the listing, and I had reduced the price twice.

I started a new job in August. I loved my job but didn't care for the long and difficult commute I had.

On that particular November morning, I was dragging myself to the train station. I was cold too. My knees would sometimes freeze to the point that I could not walk. It was also my birthday! My children were living out of Virginia, and I was alone as usual.

Other people's birthdays are often well anticipated, planned, discussed, and filled with gifts, cards, and dinners, but mine would be known only to myself, except maybe a call from my two children. It didn't seem to be a big deal for anyone else, and that got to me that morning. I complained to the Lord and explained how the weight of two mortgages, my three-hour commute to and from work every day, and my freezing bones that were hurting me—and on top of all that it was my birthday and I felt so alone and so unloved.

I am sure the Lord carefully listened to that moaning and groaning because He decided to make it up to me! That evening when I got off the train and came to my car, I found out my car wouldn't start. After a twelve-hour workday on a cold November day and a torturous train ride, now I was stuck in the parking lot! Another reason to grumble... I called a friend of mine and told him about it, and he said he would be right there. Meanwhile I continued looking up into the starry sky, and I apologized to my Lord for my complaints.

Right then the phone rang, and it was my realtor. She said that we had a buyer! I was so excited and looked up into the heavens, knowing it was God's work.

"Isn't this is a great gift for Thanksgiving?" the realtor said.

"No, silly, this is my birthday gift from the Lord!" I said excitedly. "This morning, I complained of not being loved on my birthday so much that He wanted to surprise me," I continued, as I was the laughing and crying all at the same time.

If that wasn't enough, when I got home (after my friend started my car), I saw in my mailbox a heartwarming card from my daughter who had poured her heart out to tell me how much I meant to her and to my little granddaughter.

I cried and I praised my Lord for being so compassionate and so caring that He opened the windows of heaven and lavished me with His blessings!

It Was Lost, but Now It's Found

My old house was under contract. We were ready for closing. I had a phone call from the title company that the buyer's lawyer would like to see my divorce decree. I asked why, and she said he wanted to verify the name on the title, etc. It had been about fifteen years since my divorce. I had packed up all my belongings twice before when I listed the house for sale; this time was the third time. Even when I was in my old house, I had not seen those papers for years; now, in the new house, I had no idea where it was and where to look. All I had unpacked were the things I needed for daily use. I had no clue where this paper was, what box, etc. They needed it in a day or two, and I had to go on business travel the following Monday.

I called the lady from the title company and asked, "Is this a typical request? I don't recall people asking for divorce papers since the title of the house shows the name of owner." She said it was not a typical request, and the buyer might or might not care about their lawyer's request, but if they did agree with his request, then the sale could only go through by providing this. I told her that I would try to find it but I was sure I could not since I had not seen this paper for years. My entire household was in boxes in several different rooms, and I didn't even know where to start to look. That weekend I looked everywhere I could, and at the end I gave up.

I had already surrendered to the fact that the sale might not happen, so on Sunday night I went to bed to get my rest because I needed to be at the airport at 8:00 a.m. the next day for my business travel.

That night, I woke up at about 2:00 a.m. by the power of the Holy Spirit. The Spirit directed me to my closet—a large walk-in room next to my bedroom. The Holy Spirit wanted me to look into my luggage that was wide open in the floor. It had been there for few months since I was still living in boxes. I was puzzled about why He wanted me to check the luggage since it clearly was empty except for a few odds and ends. I said, "Lord, there is nothing here; this has been empty for months."

The Holy Spirit, now more strongly, directed me to just touch the couple items that were left there. I did not understand why the Lord wanted me to check in there since I could see that there were no papers there other than a small shirt and an old sock. One could see the entire bottom of the luggage clearly. Those few items were only in one corner area. I had no choice but to obey my Lord.

I laid my hand on those items and just slightly moved my hand to the sides, just like a wave. Oh my! I saw my divorce decree folded in there by itself. The decree was not in its usual envelope or with any other papers. It was just there and in my hands!

> *He performs wonders that cannot be fathomed,*
> *miracles that cannot be counted.*
> —Job 5:9

My knees lost their strength as I realized how the Lord brought the paper to me. The fact that He was concerned about my problem while I was asleep and had decided to resolve it brought tears to my eyes. Oh, the love of the Father, I thought, was like an endless river, flowing with more power and more vigor as I hit obstacles. I felt the love of the one who wiped my tears and cuddled me in that mid-morning night! With a smile on my face and crying eyes, I went back to bed and rested on the assurance of His unfailing love.

The next morning, I put the paper in the garage and called my realtor from the airport and told her to go and get the paper and give it to the people who asked for it. She asked me on the phone how I found it. I told her that the Lord did and told her the story. She was in awe at the power of God's love for me. I told her then that He loves all the people. It is the people who reject Him who never will experience His showers of blessings!

Pray Like Jesus

I was waiting at the train station in Washington after a day of work. My heart was heavy. My daughter's condition was weighing me down. She was going through a painful divorce and was a complete wreck emotionally, physically, and spiritually. Her health was diminishing before my eyes, and her explosive emotions were unbearable. I was worried about her future and her life.

As I waited for the train on that late sunny afternoon, I spoke to the Lord of the heavens and earth. I told Him how much I needed His help and His hand in her life. I told Him, *"Lord, You didn't give her to me just to see her die in front of my eyes. You didn't give her to me just to see her suffer. I know You have a plan for her, but I am being trampled under the weight of the burden and I don't think I can bear it anymore. Lord, she needs You. I need You."*

The train came, and I boarded and found a seat. I wanted to close my eyes and rest, but the person in front of me was reading his newspaper and caught my attention. I usually cannot stand the noise of newspaper especially what the ink does to one's hands. At home, if I touched a newspaper for any reason, I had to wash my hands right away at least three times. I even detest the smell of newspaper!

Usually if there were a rider next to my seat or the one in front or back, I would get up and go somewhere else to sit, but this particular time was different. Not only did I not have the desire to get up and change my seat, but I also wanted to know what he was reading. This, I assure you, had never happened before!

I leaned forward. I was able to see and read the bolded headline: "Like Jesus, Keep Prayer a Priority." I smiled! I knew the message was for me. I knew the Lord was telling me not to stop praying. Our Savior kept on praying to the Father until the very last moments before His arrest, and even while on the cross, pouring His blood for the sake of those who had hung Him there, He prayed.

I smiled and said quietly, "Yes, Lord. I will keep on praying".

I sat back and smiled a little more, and I thanked Him for speaking to me using the *Washington Post*!

Jesus at the Wheel on I-495

My granddaughter and I are travel buddies! We travel everywhere together. She loves adventure. She is also very mature and a helpful traveler.

In April of 2009, we launched a trip to Ohio to meet the extended family of my then-to-be daughter-in-law and to attend her bridal shower. This was our first trip to Ohio, and Lily and I were excited.

I was driving, for the first time, my daughter's new car. The car was only two weeks old, so it made sense to use that rather than my old 2002 van with over ninety-eight thousand miles!

Just a short time after we departed our home, the weather changed. About forty minutes into our trip on five-lane Interstate 495, the rain started to pour. We were in the shoulder-less, leftmost lane. I could not see the cars ahead of me because of the pouring rain. The cars were coming at more than sixty-five miles per hour as if they did not have to deal with the rain issue.

Fog began to cover my windshield. I looked for the fog vent but couldn't see one. I started to stretch my hand toward the glass with a tissue, and I was able to clean it a couple of times, but quickly the fog filled the windshield, and I was driving totally blind. I could not see anything. There were no red lights in front of me that I could follow because of both the rain and the inside fog. I could hear the noise of cars on my right side mingled with the sound of thunder and pouring rain! I could not even see enough to change lanes to stop. There was no shoulder space on the left of my lane. I was surrounded with imminent danger!

I was certain, beyond any doubt, that I was going to be in a fatal accident. I was mostly thinking of Lily in the backseat. Everything was happening so fast. I had only time to say, "Jesus" in my mind. (I lost my speech; no words could come out of my throat.) All of a sudden, I saw my car changing lanes to my right without seeing anything, and in a matter of a second, I was on the most right lane—the exit lane!

The Lord stopped all the traffic on I-495 to let me go to my most right lane. I went five lanes to my right to exit the highway and to safety! How? I don't know. I just know that I was totally blind, and there were many cars zooming in that pouring rain, and I was moved to the exit lane. I found a place to stop at the exit lane, played with the panel a little, and found a way to clear the fog. I waited a few minutes to take a breath and to digest what just happened. I looked at Lily and said, "Did you see what the Lord Jesus did?" She was quiet and scared and never said a word until this moment, and then she smiled and said, "He was awesome, wasn't He?"

"He sure was," I answered, and took another deep breath, and tears welled in my eyes. I slowly continued, "And He is!"

Pastor Skip Heitzig from the Calvary Albuquerque often refers to a bumper sticker on some cars that say, "The Lord is my co-pilot," and he tells his congregation that Jesus wants the keys!

That day Jesus took the keys and the control of the wheel, and that is the only reason why Lily and I are alive today!

"Name that Book" from Thirty Thousand Feet

A few months before the writing of this book, I was flying back home from one of my business travels. We were cruising at thirty thousand feet on a nice, sunny day. As usual, I was gazing into the beautiful universe that my Father made. The clouds were white and fluffy and were formed into balls, hills, and multiple levels. I was surprised that the plane's high speed did not seem to disturb or affect the heaven's peace!

I was mesmerized and lost (intentionally) in its beauty. The feeling of contentment and satisfaction reminded me of the way I feel in my intimate moments with my Lord. Although I am usually mindful of the fact that the Holy Spirit lives in my heart, there are particular times when I can feel His divine presence next to me, and this was one of those times. Like a child who is quick to take advantage of her father's presence, I asked Him for guidance. I said, "Lord, what would you like this book's title to be since it is about You and for You?"

The rush of the fluffy white clouds outside the small plane's window toward my face was incredible! It was as if I was flying on my own wings, smiling, and enjoying my Father's glory! Quickly the Lord answered. "The name of the book will be *He Gave Me His Heart, So I Gave Him Mine.*" The whole phrase danced before my eyes on top, in the middle, and on the bottom of the clouds! I couldn't resist saying, "Wow, how profound!"

Although the memory of Him giving me His heart was far away from the present, the Lord wanted to tie that experience tightly with my day of salvation and say it all in one title! I don't know why I was surprised. I should have known He would come up with a unique and profound title like that. After all, His Word says so: "His thoughts are profound"(Ps 92:5).

I thought it was a perfect title!

"So it is," I said happily.

I Didn't Let You Go

I am embarrassed to tell you that I came so close to giving up on my daughter, but the Lord, thankfully, stopped me.

After four years of praying, assisting, discussing, and struggling, one early September, during a typical argument, she said things to me that I never thought I would ever hear from my own child.

I knew Satan was behind it, and I knew that the enemy is much bigger and more powerful than me. I was stunned and so kept quiet in my despair. A day later, I was flying out to Albuquerque for a business trip.

I was reading a book, and this particular chapter was about how Satan penetrates himself into the minds and hearts of people and keeps them from hearing the truth.

As I was reading this, my mind jumped to my daughter's state of being, and my own weariness of having witnessed it with the heartache that it brings. In my mind, I decided to "let her go." That is, I decided to let her go to Satan's side since he had a tight grip on her, and I felt like my efforts were bearing no fruit.

Suddenly I heard the Holy Spirit speak to me, "I didn't let *you* go!"

The rebuke was as loud and strong as a smack on the head, yet filled with warmth of His love! I quickly closed the book and said, "Yes, Lord. I am sorry. I won't let her go."

On my free evening the following day, I went to the Calvary Albuquerque Church, and at the end of the service, the pastor asked people who needed prayer to come forward, and the church, as the body of Christ, would pray with the individual.

I went forward and told them about the flight experience and my prayer. We prayed as the body of Christ, and we knew that He was in our midst.

When two of you gather in My Name, I will be in the midst of you.
—Matthew 18:20

We prayed for the total deliverance of my daughter and for the healing of her heart.

I came back, and since then, my daughter has changed 180 degrees! She became as lovely, kind, and sweet as I remembered her from her childhood. I waited a couple of months to see if this was truly the transformation and deliverance I had been waiting for or if it was a temporary good mood. November came, and she gave me a card for my birthday that I could not easily read it for I was crying all over it.

In one line she said, "I am so thankful that you and God didn't give up on me!"

I knew then that this was a healing and deliverance from my Savior, and it was for real!

It's been over nine months now, and I am still at awe with the power of transformation that the Lord has shown. Our family is once again intact and serving Him together.

And as for me and my family, we will serve the Lord.
—*Joshua 24:15*

I wrote a song of praise and thanksgiving upon the reflection on all the blessings that the Lord has showered on me.

Only You, Jesus

Only You, Jesus, can satisfy my hunger
For You alone are my Bread of Life
Only You, Jesus, can quench my thirst
For You alone are my Living Water

Some may call You Teacher or Rabbi
Some may call You a mere man, a prophet
But only You, Jesus, can save my soul
For You alone are my Wonderful Savior, Mighty Redeemer

Many have lost their direction in life
Many are wandering in desolate desert
They try many different ways
But only You, Jesus, are the Way, the Truth, and the Life

Many are sick, hurting, and in turmoil
They try all kinds of treatments to no avail
They put their faith in science, medicine, or luck
But only You, Jesus, are the Healer and the Prince of Peace

Many have come in Your name
Many have been lied to and deceived
Many have chosen science, religion, or this world
But only You, Jesus, are Emmanuel, the Bright Morning Star

Only You, Jesus, are the Word of God, the Lamb of God
Only You, Jesus, are the King of kings and the Lord of lords
Only You, Jesus, are the Alpha and Omega, the First and the Last
Only You, Jesus, are the Great I AM

I am still being showered by His blessings, and His blessings are new every morning.

8

TURNING STRONGHOLDS INTO REASONS TO BELIEVE

I am the gate; whoever enters through me will be saved . . .
—John 10:9

I believe that the heaviest strongholds in Islam that keep Muslims from seeing the truth can be the most crucial reasons to believe in Jesus Christ once they are broken with the power of truth.

In this chapter, I would like to engage, or rather challenge, my Muslim readers in a critical and worthwhile, as well as fun, exercise. You need to meet at least one of the following criteria:

- If Islam has left you empty, purposeless, and unexcited
- If you just want to know the meaning of life, the purpose of your life, and the ultimate truth
- If Islam has failed to show you the clear and sure way to heaven
- If you are afraid of questioning or criticizing your religion
- If you feel trapped (like a prisoner) by your religion or in your religion
- If you feel not valued or loved or are without hope
- If you never hear God speak to you, your prayers are not answered, or you see no miracles in your life

- If you are not completely sure what would happen to you if you were to die tonight

If you meet one or more of the above conditions, I invite you to an exciting and potentially life-transforming challenge that is twofold:

1. I will state the strongholds in Islam.
2. I will attempt to explain the truth about them (using the Holy Bible).

Since this book is not intended to be apologetic in its nature and purpose, I will limit the scope of evidence and the respective discussion for another time and will only highlight some relevant evidence, reasoning, and comparisons.

This is a challenge so keep up with this exercise till the end, even if you found yourself not interested in the beginning. Remember that truth will be victorious no matter how much it is challenged.

Let's start.

Stronghold 1: The Bible, "Injil," Was Written by Men, Not God, and Is Corrupted/Changed

One of the heaviest strongholds Muslims carry is in regard to the Bible and its accuracy and authenticity as the Word of God. I used to believe that the Christian Bible was written by men; I believed it was a collection of men's opinions and not God's Word. This belief impeded me from even being willing to listen to the message of Christ.

Muslims also bring up the issue of corruption. They believe since the Bible was translated into many languages, and also because it was written years after Jesus' life, then it cannot be trusted.

Since I plan to use the Bible to respond to all the strongholds below, this particular stronghold has priority on my list because all other responses are based on this one.

Moreover, I strongly believe that if this stronghold were to turn into a belief that the Holy Bible is God's Word (as it did for me), and that the Bible is inerrant, indestructible, infallible, and above all, it has power and life beyond a collection of letters, then the rest of the strongholds slowly but surely will crumble down, one by one, and turn into essential reasons to believe in Jesus Christ as Lord and Savior.

The Word of God or Man's Opinion?

The Holy Bible contains sixty-six books. The New Testament was written in approximately AD 70, that is, only about thirty years or so after Jesus' crucifixion and resurrection. The original writers were the witnesses who walked, talked, and ate with Jesus Christ. These disciples were real witnesses to the events during Jesus' ministry and until He ascended to heaven.

The Bible contains the Old Testament and the New Testament and was written over the course of approximately twenty-seven hundred years by over forty different writers of different ages, generations, backgrounds, and walks of life (fisherman, doctor, kings, tax collectors). Yet there is an undisputable consistency, coherency, and agreement throughout the books of the Bible! Only a God-authored book could survive all that diversity and variability over a long span of time.

> *All scripture is God-breathed and is useful for teaching, rebuking, correcting and training in righteousness.*
> —2 Timothy 3:16

"God-breathed" means "inspired by God" or "came out of God's mouth." God used different people, in different times, from different backgrounds to write His Word and to give it to future generations. The prophets who wrote most of the Old Testament were chosen to write God's Word, not by their own will but by God's will, gradually over the years. How do I know that the writers wrote by God's will and inspiration and not their own?

First, it is because they did not have an agenda. They were not state rebels or warriors. They did not seek power or intend to establish a religion. In fact, in the case of Moses, he gave up all his earthly power and glory to serve God. Moses grew up in the Pharaoh's kingdom, was a master over Egypt's population, and could have had all the inheritance and power of the most powerful ruler on the face of the earth, but when he was called to do God's work on earth, he became a servant. He is believed to have written the first five books of the Bible.

Second, the stories, the plan of God, the prophecies, and all historical accounts are congruent and totally in agreement. Again, these are people from different walks of life, different educations, and different generations. It is clear they did not check each other's notes! Yet God's plan for mankind's salvation is evident throughout the sixty-six books of the Bible. Only a God-breathed Word can outlast all these variables.

Before He ascended to heaven, Jesus said, "But the Helper, the Holy Spirit, whom the Father will send in My name, He will teach you all things, and bring to your remembrance all that I said to you" (John 14:26).

Jesus promised His disciples that the Holy Spirit will teach them and will remind them of all that He said and did.

Jesus Himself often referred to the Scriptures (what we call the Old Testament) to make a point or to show who He was. (He would not have done that if He knew it was not God's Word.) He even told of the Scripture's power of prophecy. Referring to the Old Testament, Jesus said:

> *Do not think that I came to abolish the Law or the Prophets; I did not come to abolish, but to fulfill. For truly I say to you, until heaven and earth pass away, not the smallest letter or stroke shall pass away from the Law, until all is accomplished (Matt 5:17-18).*

In above verse, God makes it clear that under no circumstances (time, technology, politics, natural disasters, etc.) would He allow even one small letter of the Scripture to pass away! That is, God takes responsibility for preserving His Word, and mankind cannot and will not be able to make it disappear.

In fact, many rulers of the world throughout the past two thousand years tried to destroy the Bible, but they were not successful. The Bible is indestructible because it is the Word of the true God who is sovereign over all that is in heaven and on earth and over all life!

As the matter of fact, the Bible that was in circulation in the seventh century, over six hundred years after the New Testament was written, was used by Islamic leaders, including Mohammad himself, to show validity and authenticity. The Bible that we use today is the same Bible (same content) that was in circulation in seventh century.

Here are writings from the Qur'an that show the Holy Bible was regarded as God's revelation to mankind, and more importantly, it calls it "truth" that has come "from your Lord":

> If you were in doubt as to what we have revealed unto you, then ask those who have been reading the Book from before you: the Truth has indeed come to you from your Lord: so be in no wise of those who doubt (Surah 10:94).

Islam goes against its own Qur'an when it denies that the Holy Bible has come from God and it is the truth. Islam goes against its own Qur'an when it denies Jesus, His deity, and His gift of salvation because in the passage above, it counsels its readers against doubting the "Book": "so be in no wise of those who doubt."

Is the Bible Corrupted/Changed?

Another sureh speaks of the confirmation of the Scriptures that "came before" and about safeguarding it: "To you We sent the Scriptures in truth, confirming the scripture that came before it, and guarding it in safety" (Sureh 5:48).

The Qur'an goes further than just proclaiming the truth of the Holy Bible. It also speaks of God taking responsibility to safeguard it!

So has the Bible changed or been corrupted from its original version?

No. These two surehs in Qur'an should convince Muslims that the Bible that was used in the Jewish and Christian community over six hundred years after Jesus Christ walked on earth was accepted as the truth (the Word of God) and therefore, uncorrupted.

The Bible that we have today is the exact copy of the Bible that was in distribution in seventh century. Moreover, in 1947 to mid-1950s, a few jars filled with Scriptures were found in eleven different caves near the Dead Sea, and they came to be known as the Dead Sea Scrolls. These scrolls were tested and evaluated by experts and found to be original manuscripts preserved and dated back to 150 BC. These scrolls were compared to their respective books of the Old Testament (Psalms, Isaiah, etc.) and found to be identical to today's version. This discovery and other archeological discoveries have proved to be priceless evidence on the accuracy and authenticity of the Bible that we use today.

For me personally, I had two occasions (recorded in chapter 5 and 7) when I wrote by the power and inspiration of the Holy Spirit.

The first time it caused my heart to break and become humble to the true God and led me to believe on the Son of God as my only Lord and Savior. At the time, I did not know anything about the Bible and had never been to a church, but the one and only Savior authored that poem by using me! Life, for me, was never the same again.

The second time, explained in chapter 7, was when the Holy Spirit inspired my writing of one of my candidacy questions after a prayer. I testify that I did not have the information before, and when I wrote it, I had no control over the choice of words, but I was conscious and aware of the subject matter. My hand was just a tool to write what the Spirit of God breathed. That is why I never again questioned the authenticity of the Bible as the Word of God even though men penned it.

One thing I have learned throughout my unforgettable walk with the Lord is that we, mere men, should never limit God by stating what He can or cannot do. He is an all-knowing, all-powerful, all-present God. By limiting God, we would make God in our image (what we imagine He is or what He can or cannot do). The truth is that we were made in His image. He can, has, and will do anything, natural or supernatural, to accomplish His goal. What we are told in the Bible is what He wanted us to know. What is not in the Bible does not negate the existence of God's other truths or His ability. The Bible says we cannot *fathom* God's mind. Listen to these few verses:

> *Great is the LORD and most worthy of praise;*
> *his greatness no one can fathom.*
> —Psalm 145:3

Can you fathom the mysteries of God? Can you probe the limits of the Almighty? They are higher than heavens-what can you do?

> *They are deeper than the depths of the grave—what can you know?*
> *Their measure is longer than the earth and wider than the sea.*
> —Job 11:7

> *Do you not know? Have you not heard? The LORD is the everlasting*
> *God, the Creator of the ends of the earth. He will not grow tired*
> *and weary, and his understanding no one can fathom.*
> —Isaiah 40:28

Stronghold 2: Jesus Is a Mere Prophet, Not the Son of God

I know the Qur'an teaches that Jesus was just a prophet and absolutely rejects the theology behind the Son of God (Q: 112, 5:17). As I said in previous chapters, Satan uses God's truth and then distorts it, manipulates it and makes sure people are kept in the dark about the true identity of Jesus, or else they would believe in Him as their Savior, and by that, they would ruin Satan's goal of taking them with him to the lake of fire for all eternity.

Satan tells people, especially Muslims, that Jesus was a mere messenger or prophet when in fact He was more than a prophet. He was Lord and the only Savior of the world. He was more than a son of Mary. He was the only begotten Son of God. He was more than a priest or rabbi. He was the High Priest—the Holy One. He was more than a good and peace-loving man. He was the Prince of Peace and the Maker of heaven and earth. He was more than a teacher. He was the all-knowing God. He was more than a man. He was the Word of God who came down from heaven, voluntarily was "squeezed" in humanity, and dwelled among us.

The truth is the truth, no matter how many millions of people disagree! Even if the whole world were to believe what Islam (or Mormonism, Jehovah's Witnesses, Hinduism, or Buddhism) teaches, it makes absolutely no difference to God, although it saddens Him, for He does not desire for any to perish. (See 2 Pet 3:9.)

Islam believes that the notion of "Son of God" implies that God had sexual intercourse with Mary and had a son. But this is not what the Holy Bible teaches. God is Spirit, and Jesus is the Word of God who took the form of man and walked among us for a short thirty-three years.

In the beginning was the Word, and the Word was with God, and the Word was God . . . "And the Word became flesh and dwelt among us."
—John 1:1-2

Pastor Skip Heitzig describes the uniqueness of Jesus this way:

> Infinity became finite. The invisible now is visible. Eternity is now squeezed into time. The supernatural is confined by the natural. Or if you please, God just moved into our neighborhood for thirty-three years. "The Word became flesh."

God the Father uses relationships familiar to mankind to speak to men and to display His divine character as trinity (more on this follows).

Truth does not change based on what people or even the majority of people think. God's plan goes forward no matter how much Muslims or other nonbelievers argue about this issue. The best way to proceed is to have an open mind and look at the evidence.

Here are but a few pieces of hard evidence:

- Jesus was born of a virgin. There has never been a baby born of a virgin girl ever in history of mankind.
- The Spirit of God came upon the Virgin Mary. That is, no other human being was a party to this unusual conception! Even the Qur'an acknowledges this. (See sureh Q 3:45-47.)
- The Angel of God brought the good news to the shepherds, and told them: "I bring you Good News; Today, in the city of David, a Savior is born" (Luke 2:11).
- Jesus' birth was foretold by the prophet Isaiah four hundred years before he was born! Here is the verse:

> *For unto us a child is born, a son is given and the government will be on his shoulders, and his name shall be Wonderful Counselor, Everlasting Father, Prince of Peace (Isa 9:6).*

- The Father introduces Jesus as His Son. God said, "This is my beloved Son, in whom I am well pleased" (Matt. 3:16).
- Jesus introduces Himself as the Son of God. In Luke 22:70, Jesus was asked, "Are you the Son of God?" Jesus said, "I AM."
- Jesus said, in John 9:30, "I and the Father are one."

- Jesus was sinless. The only way to be sinless is to be more than a human being, more than a prophet. Only God is sinless and therefore holy. So Jesus was God!
- Jesus, during His short life on earth, forgave people's sins. Only God can forgive sins. Ironically, the Qur'an acknowledges that only God can forgive sins. So Jesus was God.
- Jesus brought back the dead by calling the dead. Only God can bring back to life after they have died. In Luke 7:12-15 it is written, "As he approached the town gate, a dead person was being carried out-the only son of his mother, and she was a widow. And a large crowd from the town was with her. When the Lord saw her, his heart went out to her and he said, 'Don't cry.' Then he went up and touched the coffin, and those carrying it stood still. He said, 'Young man, I say to you, get up!' The dead man sat up and began to talk, and Jesus gave him back to his mother."
- Jesus was the only one who opened the eyes of the blind, As John 9:32 says, "Since the world began it has been unheard of that anyone opened the eyes of one who was born blind." Matthew 20:34 records, "Jesus had compassion on them and touched their eyes. Immediately they received their sight and followed him."
- He was resurrected and appeared to His disciples and also to more than five hundred other people for forty days before He ascended to heaven! In the legal courts today (even in an Islamic court) having only two witnesses to an event is enough for the judge to rule according to what witnesses claim. Post resurrection, more than five hundred people saw Jesus after His death and burial in His glorified body. He even asked Thomas, his doubtful disciple, to touch His side and touch His nail-pierced hands. Thomas did just that, and said, "You are Lord, God!" In Luke 16:31 is written, "But he said to him, If they do not hear Moses and the prophets, neither will they be persuaded though one rise from the dead."

Truly, Jesus was more than a prophet, more than a son of Mary; He was and is the Son of God, the very God, the King of kings and the Lord of lords, the one and only Savior of the world, and the Great I AM!

Stronghold 3: The Trinity—God Is One, Not Three!

There is no doubt that the theology of trinity is difficult to grasp even for Christians who have the knowledge of the Bible and its teachings. We humans are limited in our understanding of supernatural because we live in a "natural" world.

Pastor Skip of Albuquerque, New Mexico, puts it this way, "Natural resists supernatural." He continues, "We who are confined to the natural often struggle with the supernatural." That said the Bible makes it very clear that God is a triune God, and He reigns as the Father, the Son, and the Holy Spirit—three persons, one God.

Most of us have no problem understanding and believing that a human being has a body, mind, and spirit. We understand that we can lose a leg, have a heart transplant, change our skin color, but none of these changes would change who we really are. A dead person looks like a sleeping person, except life is not in him. That life was the spirit that is no longer there. The body and the mind are still there as tangible objects, but there is no life. Muslims, like many others, believe that when a person dies, his spirit will live, and it is only the body and mind that they bury underground.

Most people understand the "trinity" of human beings. They do believe that there is something intrinsically different with human beings than with all other living creatures. The body, mind (sometimes it is called soul), and spirit all exist in the nature of man, and man is not complete or cannot exist without one.

Muslims have no problem understanding or believing that water can exist in three different states or manifestations—liquid, gas, and solid. Yet any of those manifestations has the same essence (nature) of H2O, hydrogen and oxygen.

Muslims (especially Iranians) are very good mathematicians. They have no problem understanding or believing that a triangle has three distinct angles, without which it cannot exist as a triangle, and every angle has a role and a purpose, but together, the three angles form a single triangle, one entity.

Speaking of math, Muslims have no problem distinguishing the difference between $1+1+1=3$ and $1*1*1=1^3= 1$.

Muslims also believe that God is infinite, incomprehensible, and unlimited, and that the human mind cannot ever understand Him fully.

They also believe that God can do whatever He pleases! Couldn't that assertion include coming to earth, entering the human race—His own creation—as a man, and yet remaining God? But they refuse to even entertain the possibility of a triune God.

As I said earlier in the beginning of this chapter, I will use God's own Word to justify Christians' belief about the triune God.

Jesus, before He ascended to heaven, told His disciples, "Go and make disciples of all nations, and baptize them in the name of the Father, and of the Son and of the Holy Spirit" (Matt 28:19).

The Qur'an, in fact, teaches God, the Word, and the Spirit of God (see sureh 3:45). The Qur'an acknowledges, "the Word became Jesus." But conveniently, it refuses to accept what the Bible teaches about the triune nature of God.

The following verse displays the three persons of the trinity as present at the beginning of Jesus' ministry, distinct yet equal:

> *When He had been baptized, Jesus came up immediately from water; and behold, the heavens were opened to Him, and He saw the Spirit of God descending like a dove and lighting on Him. And suddenly a voice came from Heaven saying, "This is My beloved Son, in whom I am well pleased" (Matt 3:16-17).*

In regard to the trinity, Satan is after the Son again! Satan knows that believing in Jesus—the Son—will save every human being from the hell, and this causes him (Satan) to lose completely to God. But misery wants company! Satan wants to take down with him as many souls as possible. This is a clever plot by him to make sure the Qur'an doesn't "permit" believing the Trinity of God. God, Word, and spirit are OK but not God, Son, and Spirit. This is a deliberate plot to deceive the people God loves and wants saved.

Stronghold 4: The Crucifixion

Sureh 4:157 states, "That they said (in boast), 'We killed Christ Jesus, the son of Mary, the messenger of Allah,' but they killed him not, nor crucified him, but so it was made to appear to them, and those who differ therein are full of doubts, with no (certain) knowledge, but only conjecture to follow, for of a surety they killed him not."

The Qur'an, which came to its existence about AD 632, denies the crucifixion of Christ. This event was recorded in manuscripts for over six centuries! There are hundreds of Christian and non-Christian manuscripts (for example, Josephus, the Jewish historian of the first century), in addition to the original writings of the New Testament written by the four of the disciples who were witnesses to this unforgettable event!

The crucifixion event wasn't like any other routine crucifixion. The sky darkened, and an earthquake shook the very ground where the Roman governor lived, the very ground where the Jewish priests accused Jesus of blasphemy, the very ground where the Jews, for centuries, worshipped YHWH and awaited the Messiah. The stones, grounds, and walls of the temple broke in pieces. The veil that separated the Holy of Holies from the sin-drenched people tore from top to the bottom, signifying our direct and unveiled access to the throne of God because of the one who was hung on the cross.

> *Then, behold, the veil of the temple was torn in two from top to bottom; and earth quaked, and the rocks were split.*
> —Matthew 27:51

Satan, the dark force behind Islam, hides Jesus' death on the cross because it provided the atonement for sin. The sacrifice of Jesus provided the only way to be reconciled back to God! Satan does whatever possible to prevent this reconciliation; he wants as many souls as possible. One way to prevent people from going to God's side is to deceive them. He puts doubts in people's minds; he establishes a religion of fear, violence, and hate. Not believing in Jesus' crucifixion and atonement of sin at the cross and His resurrection is what Satan wants.

Jesus, as He took His last breathe on the cross, said, "It is finished" (John 19:30). The work of redemption was finished. He paid for the sins of mankind in full.

Jesus said, "Father, into your hands I commit my spirit" (Luke 23:46), and He expired.

Satan does not want Muslims to know that they have a Savior who *finished* the job of redeeming them! Satan does not even want them to know that Islam is his work. He wants to keep the truth of life hidden from as many people as possible. Islam, driven by the dark spirit of Satan, denies the atonement of sin because if it didn't, it could not justify the need for Islam, the Qur'an, Mohammed, or any other prophet.

The job of rescuing human beings from eternal hell is finished. His body was broken for us, and His blood was shed to pay the punishment for our sins. None of us could save ourselves. No amount of good work is good enough. We all have lied. We all have dishonored our parents. We all have forgotten to love God with all our heart and minds. We all have put other people ahead of God and therefore sinned. This is the least. We still have the sinful nature that we have to fix before we can expect to be reunited with God. We absolutely and urgently need a Savior. No one can save us because all human beings are sinners, even noble people or prophets. The only sinless person on earth was Jesus, and that is because He was God confined in flesh. His blood for sacrifice was acceptable to God because He was sinless and holy.

He, being the Lord who loved us enough to come down to earth to rescue us, told us in advance that He is the only way! He also told us that no one could be saved under any other name!

> *I am the way, the truth and the life. No one comes to the Father except through me.*
> —John 14:6

> *Salvation is found in no one else, for there is no other name under heaven given to men by which we must be saved.*
> —Acts 4:12

Stronghold 5: The Resurrection

The Qur'an does not agree that Jesus was resurrected from the dead. It does, however, state that God raised Him to heaven. Why?

Satan, as I stated in previous chapters, takes what is true and manipulates it, distorts it, or cuts it in pieces so it cannot be called true anymore. This way he deceives people with yet another version, another way to think. If Qur'an had agreed that Jesus was resurrected from the dead, it would, by default, agree that He died. Qur'an does not want to accept His death on the cross because it does not want people to know that their debts have been paid in full by His blood. People would know the true way to be forgiven and saved and to have eternal life with God—a dream come true! But for Satan, this knowledge is a nightmare!

In Luke 24:46-48, Jesus says, "This is what is written: The Christ will suffer and rise from the dead on the third day, and repentance and forgiveness of sins will be preached in his name to all nations, beginning at Jerusalem. You are witnesses of these things."

In Acts 1:3, the apostle Paul writes, "After his suffering, he showed Himself to these men and gave many convincing proofs that he was alive. He appeared to them over a period of forty days and spoke about the kingdom of God."

Christianity exploded in the world following the resurrection of Christ. People followed the risen Christ, and Christianity spread around the world, not by the sword but by the love that God expressed through His Son's birth, death on the cross, and resurrection in order to save mankind from the lake of fire or eternity in hell.

Stronghold 6: The Sin

In Iran, when we had a near-impossible petition *(nazr)*, a thanksgiving occasion, such as a loved one coming for a visit from far away, or a wedding of a son or daughter, we would sacrifice a lamb (or a goat if we couldn't get a lamb).

My father couldn't bring himself to kill the animal, so he would ask another male family member. The one in charge of buying the sacrificial lamb would look for a young, most healthy one, one without any wound, blemish, or illness. Never would he pick a sick animal—one that had some handicap, wound, or spots (due to disease). A sick, wounded, or imperfect animal would be *haram* or *unkosher*. The belief was that God would not honor or accept the petition if the lamb was not perfect. Only the best is good enough for God. This tradition, like so many other traditions, came to Islam from the Jewish biblical and cultural traditions.

I remember vividly that when the lamb would see the knife, he would put his head down in an attitude of submission. Before slaughtering, the lamb would be given water.

Most of us wouldn't stay to watch this act. It was so difficult to see the poor animal bleed to death so we can have nourishment for our bodies and enjoy our party.

The sacrificial lamb had to be killed in a way that the blood would shed. This is what is known in Jewish community as kosher and in Islamic community as *halal*.

The sacrifice for nazr intended to win favor from God because people, in their present state (with sin), were not good enough for God (not pure enough, righteous enough, sinless enough). An innocent lamb was good enough for our righteous God.

The Qur'an does not speak much about sin. We as Muslims grew up believing that it is the sins we commit as adults that cause us to anger God and be thrown in the hellfire. It is for this reason that the Qur'an and Hadith spend much effort to say that people can earn their eternity by "killing the infidels," going to Mecca, doing prayers five times a day, and giving *zakat*, the alms. This would tip the scales of good deed versus bad deeds in favor of good deeds. Even then, the Qur'an teaches that Allah may or may not forgive and accept us (Q 2:284). The Qur'an leaves the person hanging about how one can be sure one's sins are forgiven.

How is it possible that Allah may forgive even with the presence of sin (bad deeds)?

I asked this of a Muslim friend once, and he said, "The basis of forgiveness is Allah's mercifulness." I noted that holiness is also God's nature! He cannot have sin in His presence because He is holy! His mercifulness does not cancel, negate, or eliminate His holiness. His nature is unchangeable!

He understood that his logic—that is the Qur'an's logic—is flawed.

If this weren't enough of a problem, I told my friend that the Qur'an also fails to mention the problem of inherent sin, the sin that entered our human nature (our DNA) long ago through Adam and Eve and each one of us carry it in our lives from birth.

Adam and Eve sinned by disobeying God in the Garden of Eden, and thus sin entered human race. That is why God, despite the fact that up to this point He had a close, intimate fellowship with the first man and woman, drove them out because they could no longer be in His presence.

Here is God's account of how sin entered human race:

> Now the serpent was more crafty than any of the wild animals the LORD God had made. He said to the woman, "Did God really say, 'You must not eat from any tree in the garden?'" The woman said to the serpent, "We may eat fruit from the trees in the garden, but God did say, 'You must not eat fruit from the tree that is in the middle of the garden, and you must not touch it, or you will die.'" "You will not surely die," the serpent said to the woman. "For God knows that when you eat of it your eyes will be opened, and you will be like God, knowing good and evil." When the woman saw that the fruit of the tree was good for food and pleasing to the eye, and also desirable for gaining wisdom, she took some and ate, she also gave some to her husband who was with her and he ate it (Gen 3:1-6).

So we are sinners, and no amount of good deeds can erase the stain of sin on our nature's garment. Jesus tells us that if we get angry with our brother, it is like committing a murder! I don't thinks there is anyone on earth, including Muslims, who can claim never having been angry with anyone. God says, "Thou shall not lie." I don't think anyone, including Muslims, can claim to not having ever lied. So we all are sinners and therefore dead on arrival!

God says in His Word that our righteousness is like a filthy rag. That means our best deeds are filthy to Him! That is why no amount of good deeds will be able to cleanse us. God knew this, and because He does not desire for us to perish, He came to our rescue!

In the Holy Bible, *Injil*, God executes His plan to save human beings from their sins so they can enter His presence.

How?

He did it by giving us His Son, Jesus. Jesus came to earth to save. His name means, "God who saves." He paid for our sins by His shed blood. He became the Lamb of God who was sacrificed for us once and for all.

Since He was God, He was the perfect and sufficient sacrifice. At the cross at His last breath He said, "It is finished." The work of the atonement of sin was finished. Three days later, just as Jesus Himself foretold to His disciples, He rose from the dead, appeared to over five hundred people, including His disciples, and after He gave them the Great Commission (see Matt. 28:19), He ascended into heaven!

> *Neither is there salvation in any other: for there is no other name under heaven given among men whereby we must be saved.*
> —Acts 4:12

I heard a true story some years ago in the United States about a father who confessed to a murder he knew his son had committed. He knew if his son was convicted and found guilty, the wages (the sentence) would be death. He loved his son so much that he couldn't bear the thought of losing him. At the same time, something had to be done to pay for the son had done, so the father went to the police station and claimed he had done it. He took the son's sin upon himself and was put in jail. He waited for his trial that he knew would bring a death sentence. He did it because he knew his son couldn't save his own life and because he loved him so much that he willingly gave his own life so his son could be free and live.

That is precisely what God the Father did! Without a doubt, we sinners would be dead and separated from God for all eternity. The Bible says, "The wages of sin is death." We could not do enough good to become pure and sinless and in His image again.

But He loved us so much that He gave His only begotten Son to pay our penalty, just like the father in above example did. Jesus became the Lamb of God. His blood was poured to redeem us, only if we accept it. Our sins are washed away by the shed blood of Jesus. There is no other way to be forgiven and saved. Jesus is the *only* way.

> *Jesus said to him, "I am the way, the truth, and the life: no man comes unto the Father but by me."*
> —John 14:6

Stronghold 7: Leaving Islam

The last major stronghold is in regard to one's "Muslim-ness." No one dares to even think of leaving Islam for another faith. That act is a treason and punishable by death, but during the past thirty years, thanks to the Iran's Islamic Revolution exposing Islam, thousands of young and middle-aged Iranians have chosen to leave Islam and to embrace Christ, even with all its catastrophic risk.

I went to a Ukraine mission trip back in October, and I met with so many Iranians who were thirsty and hungry for the truth! New believers told me that they had never felt this excited about God before! An Iranian pastor told me that there was a couple who had come to Ukraine to vacation and maybe to stay (if they could get asylum somewhere in the world). This pastor shared the love of Jesus with the couple and invited them for Sunday worship. They were so amazed of what they heard about Jesus that they cancelled their return trip to Iran and stayed another week to hear more. The pastor told me that on the following week, the husband and wife both decided to give their hearts to Christ!

Some of the Iranian Muslims who secretly leave Islam and accept Christ wait patiently several months, and sometimes years, to leave the country to go to a neighboring country just to get baptized!

I came back with praises and thanksgiving for what the Lord is doing in the hearts and lives of these new Christians. They all praise the Lord for giving them a second chance to hear the truth!

In addition to the above hard strongholds, there is a soft stronghold that is worth discussing, and that is the cultural stronghold. Many Muslims believe that they cannot follow Jesus Christ because they are Arabs or Iranians and therefore Muslim! This is what Satan uses to hold your mind captive! Christ is not a Western Lord; He is the Lord over all the earth! Before His ascension to heaven, Jesus told His disciples, "Go to the world and make disciples [followers] of all nations."

In John 3:16, we read, "God so loved the world that He gave His only begotten Son . . ."

He loved the world, not just America, Europe, or Israel.

Later in John 3:16 it continues, "That whoever believes in Him shall not perish." "Whoever" means anyone, black, white, brown, oriental, Arab, Persian, educated, uneducated, rich, poor, sick, healthy—anyone.

Thirty-one years ago, when the Islamic Revolution of Iran occurred and the country's foundation (constitutions, laws, philosophy on justice, morality, etc.) was changed to the Islamic Republic, many soft strongholds began to break.

I remember that, pre-revolution, very few people could even think of the idea of changing citizenship. Iranians are very nationalistic. They have a long, solid heritage, and they are extremely proud of that. Becoming a citizen of another country, specially denouncing your original citizenship, was not only unnecessary but also a taboo, something that was worse than death. It was treason, very shameful, and full of disgrace.

But when the Islamic Revolution occurred and millions of Iranians escaped the religious and political persecution or left for social and economic reasons, they came face to face with issues of asylum, refugee, green card (residency), and citizenship. Those who went to America or Europe were proud to show off their new passports. Their family and friends in Iran were envious of them for carrying foreign passports and for benefitting from those foreign citizenships. This soft stronghold broke loose, and now, after thirty years, no one in Iran thinks of it as a stigma or as a betrayal.

Friends, no amount of reasons will cause God to change His standards and His plan. A coworker of mine once said, "So, it's not our fault that Adam and Eve were deceived and brought sin into us."

Because of His holiness, God will not have any sinner in His presence, unless he or she is washed in the blood of Christ, our sacrificial Lamb who takes away the sin of the world. There is no other way that a person can be saved from eternal damnation.

My hope and prayer is that if you don't know Jesus as your Savior, you spend some time pondering over these strongholds and their associated explanations of truth.

If you are led to make the decision to receive and follow Jesus Christ, you can pray the below prayer out of your heart to God and ask to be forgiven of your sins and to be saved from eternal separation from Him.

Pray to Receive Jesus as Your Lord and Savior

Lord Jesus, I recognize that I am a sinner. I ask you to forgive me. I invite you to my heart and to my life. I now know that you came from Heaven and died on the cross for my sins and you were raised on the third day to the Father. I thank you Lord, for saving me. In Your Name I pray, Amen.

Congratulations! The Bible says when even one sinner is saved, the whole of heaven rejoices and sings praises! (See Luke 15:7.) You just started a party in heaven!

My Personal Prayer

It is my fervent desire and most wholehearted passion to pray to my Father in heaven in the precious name of His Son and my Lord and Savior that once again Iran would come face to face with the God of Daniel and believe that He is the sovereign, unchanging, and eternal God.

I pray that the Lord would raise up wise leaders in today's Iran (*Ilam* or Persia in the Bible) where it would become, once again, an instrument of the Lord and for the Lord, set to honor and glorify Him just as it did 500 BC.

> *King Darius wrote to all the people, nations and men of every language throughout the land: May you prosper greatly! I issue a decree that in every part of my kingdom people must fear and*

reverence the God of Daniel. For He is the living God and He endures forever; His kingdom will never end. He rescues and He saves; He performs signs and wonders in the heavens and on the earth. He has rescued Daniel from the power of the lions.

—Daniel 6:25-27

Made in the USA
Coppell, TX
29 November 2019